Toothbrush
and other plays

A collection of 30 five-minute plays
created and performed by
Palestinian children

Toothbrush
and other plays

A collection of 30 five-minute plays
created and performed by
Palestinian children

Edited by
Nick Bilbrough

G

GILGAMESH

Toothbrush and other plays

A collection of 30 five-minute plays created and performed by Palestinian children

I would like to acknowledge the support of Andy Hockley, Jan Patterson, Melissa Scott, Scott Thornbury and Tim Sayer [HUP board of trustees], all the judges of the competition, and UNRWA and Palestinian Ministry of Education supervisors and teachers. For her generous support in all the layout and design work of this book I would like to thank Eva Afifah.

Huge thanks to all the Palestinian children who submitted plays for the competition. You are an enormous source of inspiration to us all!

Published by Gilgamesh Publishing 2019
Email: info@gilgameshpublishing.co.uk
www.gilgamesh-publishing.co.uk
ISBN 978-1-908531-83-568
© The Hands Up Project
Cover photo by Abdallah Alhaj
Design by Eva Afifah

Contents

Chapter 3: Freedom

Chapter 4: Imagination

• • •

This book is dedicated to Simon Greenall, 1954-2018

*Simon was a long-term supporter of English language
education in Palestine and main sponsor
of the HUP playwriting competition.
For this we are eternally grateful.*

Foreword
by Scott Thornbury

Drama in the English language classroom ticks all the right boxes. Especially in the way it is represented in this collection of plays that were written and performed – both live and online – by schoolchildren in Gaza and the West Bank.

Drama is participatory – it involves children working together at every stage of its production, from writing to final performance. And a lot of this participation will occur in English, since that it is the language of the final product. It is also interactive – drama involves a communicative to-and-fro which replicates real-life interaction. And, clearly, it is oral. It activates the speaking skills: at the level of pronunciation, particularly stress and intonation, and at the levels of both accuracy and fluency: the fact that drama evolves as a written text at first, which goes through successive stages of rehearsal and performance, ensures that at each iteration the spoken form becomes more polished and more fluid. It is also aural: it activates listening skills, both between the performers themselves, and on the part of the audience. Because it is enacted and contextualized, the listening process is constantly supported by non-verbal means: props, costume, set, music, gesture and movement.

More importantly still, drama is expressive: it invests an imagined world with the thoughts, experiences, feelings, fears and hopes of its creators. In the context of Palestine, this is an incredibly important function – it provides a means of thinking the unthinkable, of saying the unsayable, of dreaming the undreamable. And it is transformative: it empowers its creators by enhancing their English skills, and hence giving them a powerful voice in the wider world. But also, by construing their lives as narratives that can be performed and shared, drama eloquently affirms their identity as Palestinians and as global citizens.

Preface

Matthias Schmale, Director UNRWA Gaza

Ever since arriving in Gaza in October last year I have been deeply impressed by the creative talent I have witnessed among the 278,000 children attending our 275 UNRWA schools. Despite facing numerous hardships in their daily lives – electricity for just 4 hours a day, no access to safe drinking water etc – many children have maintained an incredible zest for life and learning. And as some of the plays contained in this book demonstrate, there is extraordinary writing talent to be found amongst them. The manner in which they express their deepest feelings, dreams and experiences is both touching and inspirational. I have been privileged to see some of the children – and in particular girls – act out their own plays. They are not just good at writing but also at performing! Like children everywhere in the world, they surely deserve not only the right to a decent education but the opportunities to use that education to achieve a more dignified way of life. UNRWA is very grateful to the Hands Up Project for giving at least some of Gaza's Palestinian refugee children the chance to get a few steps closer to realising their hopes for a better future.

Introduction

At the end of 2017 The Hands Up Project launched a playwriting competition for Palestinian children aged 15 or younger, attending UNRWA or Ministry of Education Schools in Gaza and the Occupied West Bank. The task was to create an original play in English that could be performed in a maximum of five minutes, by a maximum of five actors. Participants were asked to submit both the script of their play and a video recording of them acting it.

A panel of 25 judges, including actors, theatre directors and education specialists from Palestine and around the world were then asked to assess the plays, and the winning group was invited to spend a week in the UK, performing their play at the Hands Up Project conference at Westminster University in London, and at various schools and theatres.

A total of eighty-eight plays were submitted for the competition, the vast majority of which were from UNRWA schools in Gaza. Out of these, 13 plays went forward to the final and these were all awarded the following specific prizes :

- Inner Thoughts   Best overall play

- Window onto the Outside   Best play about Gaza

- Live Your Life   Best universal play

- Unity Play   Best parable play

- When Will the Sun Rise?   Best play from the West Bank

- I Have A Dream   Best filmed play

- Hope; Tomorrow is a Better Day   Best fantasy play

- Beyond the Gate .... Best play about the blockade

- Toothbrush .... Most creative play

- Stolen dreams .... Best play about childhood

- My mother-in-law is .... Best comedy
  a Troublemaker

- Hope .... Best boys play

- Us and them .... Best documentary play

All of these 13 finalists are included in this collection as well as 17 other excellent plays that were submitted, fitting into the four themes of family, school, freedom and imagination. The themes are a good way to organise the book but having them does mean that unfortunately some very good plays had to be excluded.

The Play's the Thing

Hamlet:

I'll have grounds

More relative than this—the play's the thing

Wherein I'll catch the conscience of the King.

Hamlet Act 2, scene 2, 603–605

Hamlet was right of course when he spoke those immortal lines: a play is indeed an excellent vehicle by which the conscience of the audience may be stirred. He decided to put on 'The murder of Gonzago' [the play within the play in Hamlet] because the plot had similarities with the actual murder of his father. Suspecting that his uncle, Claudius, was guilty of the murder, he wanted to observe Claudius watching the play to see if he could detect his conscience being stirred.

These plays, similarly, are an excellent way to raise awareness about life in Palestine – a context with a cultural heritage which has been ignored, denied even, by many Governments and by large sections of the world's media. They touch on issues such as the occupation, the blockade of Gaza, human rights violations and shortages of electricity and other basic needs, but they're also a celebration of the very rich Palestinian culture and of its creativity. They provide a fascinating, and sometimes heart-breaking, insight into the world as viewed through the eyes of Palestinian children, but at the same time there is something very universal about many of the themes explored.

The videos of these plays have already been viewed by many thousands of people around the world on our Youtube playlist *Bit.ly/HUPPlaysList*, but the children who created them, and their teachers, would also be very honoured if the scripts were read and used by as many people, in as many different contexts, as possible. If you are a teacher of learners of English as a foreign or second language you might like to consider working with some of them as scripts to read and perform.

Of course, if we put on a play with learners of English as a foreign language, we're focussing principally on how the participants can benefit from the experience rather than the audience. As the acclaimed drama in education expert, Dorothy Heathcote, put it [Wagner 1999], 'The difference between theatre and classroom drama is that in theatre everything is contrived so that the audience gets the kicks. In the classroom, the participants get the kicks.' So what kind of kicks can second language learners get from rehearsing and performing a play?

Some language learning benefits of acting in a short play

1. Many coursebooks present language in lexical sets *(colours, or adjectives to describe people etc)*, but research into language retention (see for example Folse 2004) suggests that new language is more memorable for

learners when it's presented in meaningful contexts with a clear theme. Scripts can provide such contexts very well. In the first script included here, **'Mother's day'**, for example, grammar, vocabulary and chunks of language related to the theme of parent/child conversations occurs naturally, and in relation to each other *(I've been +ing.., homework, tidy your room, proud of you etc)*.

2. Although most learners prioritise being able to speak over being able to write in a language, it's notoriously difficult for learners to notice the features of spoken language. Whereas written language can be accessed in the timeframe of the reader, the listener has no such control over speech; once words have been spoken, unless they are recorded in some way, they simply disappear. Scripts are effectively spoken language written down, and therefore provide the best of both worlds.

3. Of course, we express ourselves and our ideas not just through the words that we use. Communication is an embodied experience [Thornbury 2013] and we also create meanings with facial expressions, with gestures and with physical movements. When performing a play, it's important to include all of these features, alongside and in conjunction with language, in order to make the play realistic. Incorporating physicality helps us to remember the lines for performing the play, but it also helps the language to stick in long term memory long after the play has taken place.

4. It's not what you say, it's the way that you say it! A lot of meaning is carried through pronunciation, but it's hard to get this point across to learners when spoken language is practised in isolation, and without a wider context. When practising the lines of a play, as teachers we can discuss with the learners different ways of saying the lines and the impact that this has. More importantly they can feel

it themselves through other people's reactions to what they say.

5. Practising and performing a play provides the perfect combination of very controlled and very free language use. Learning the lines involves lots of repetition of a model of natural English, but at the same time there is the potential for plenty of freer discussion around how to say the lines, how to block the scene, the use of costumes etc. Both of these types of language use can help to develop fluency. As well as this. It can be very useful to involve an element of improvisation into the process of learning lines itself. If the script is sometimes taken away and learners improvise using whatever language they have available to them it helps them to both remember the lines and to personalise them.

6. In order to learn any new word, chunk of language or grammatical structure, learners need to practice it lots of times. A few hours of English a week isn't really enough time for this practice to be effective, so learners need to take it away with them and do it in their own time. As teachers we want them to be turning new language over in their minds at any opportune moment. Getting ready to perform a play can provide the level of practice needed in a much more meaningful way than the coursebook can usually offer – not just practice for the sake of it, but practice to make the most accomplished performance possible.

7. Sometimes in ELT methodology we tend to shy away from the idea of performance. We avoid putting learners on the spot and incorporate lots of pair and group work so that learners feel safe and unthreatened. This is all very well and can certainly help to build learners confidence, but so too can incorporating a performance stage in my opinion. There is a big difference of course between

performing something when you are unprepared, and performing when you've got to the point where you feel comfortable about what you are doing. For many learners it is the performance stage which provides the push they need in order to make real progress.

If you do end up making a video of any of the plays, of your own adaptations of them, or perhaps of your own play inspired by one of them, then please do get in touch with us at info@handsupproject.org. I'm sure that young people in Palestine would love to see what you come up with, and it could be that we can arrange a live link-up with the original authors so that you can share your versions with each other remotely.

Nick Bilbrough, August 2018

References

Folse, K [2004] Vocabulary Myths; University of Michigan Press

Shakespeare, W [1603] Hamlet

Thornbury, S [2013] 'The Learning Body' in Meaningful Action by Arnold J and Murphey,T [eds]; CUP

Wagner, B [1999] Dorothy Heathcote: Drama as a learning medium; Calendar islands publishers

Chapter 1

Family

Palestinian society is very family oriented and this was strongly reflected in the large number of plays submitted for the competition which were about family relationships. **Mother's day** and **Pottery and Rain** are about the challenges of parenting and how, as a mother or father, it's almost impossible to get it right all the time. In **Sa'sa and Ma'ma** and **The fighter** we see some examples of the power of parents to hold a family together in difficult circumstances, and in **Unity Play** and **My mother-in-law is a troublemaker** some ways in which family conflict may be resolved. **The Golden Lira** and **Live your life** focus on the tensions that can arise as children start to grow up, and as they, and others, start to think about what the future might bring.

Mother's Day

'Mother's Day' was written and performed by Raya Mutasem Abu Ayyash, Dania Mahmoud Bragheth, Ruba Sameer Abu Sarah, Doua' Mahmoud Toma, Lojyn Hussen Al Omari and Sarah Yousef Abu Sarah from Zahreat Al Madhean basic school for girls, Hebron with support from their teacher Asma M Qadi. A recording of the play, performed by the actors is available here...

https://youtu.be/w8dDSVRGZbc

Scene. The mother is cleaning the house and singing. Boy 1 is playing computer games. Another boy comes in.

Boy 2: Mum, what's for lunch today?

Mum: Well...

Boy 2: *[interrupting]* Oh cookies! I like cookies *[he rushes to the cookies tin on the table].*

Mum: *[angry]* Stop! Don't eat cookies! Since the early morning I've been cooking for you.

I've cooked chicken for you. I've made vegetable soup ... *[She freezes]*

Narrator: *[coughs]* Well, I'm the narrator. So, you can see that Mums don't always know the right words to say, or how to say things in the right way. Take for example what has just happened here. Really what mum is trying to say is 'Eat vegetables because vegetables will make you healthy and strong'. Please audience, keep watching.

Mum leaves the older boy and goes to the younger one.

Mum: Hey you! Stop playing computer games. You spend most of the time on this thing. Get up. Do something else instead of this *[she makes him move his feet, so she can clean under him. Then she makes him get up and pushes him into his room]* Go to your room and do your homework. Don't sit there or you will die! *[pointing to the seat where he was before]*

The mother freezes

Narrator: You see! She did it again in the heat of the moment. Mums can sound mean but what this Mum is really trying to say is just, 'Find a useful way to spend your time. Don't just play. Have time to play but do your homework as well because education stimulates your mind and increases your intelligence, as you know.' Watch on, dear audience ....

[The mother continues with her house work again. Another boy comes into the house with a scruffy appearance]

Boy 3: Hey Ma! …. Ma! Ma!

Mum : What?

Boy 3: *[gesturing]* What's up?

Mum : *[mocking him]* What's up? Don't you go to school to learn proper ways to speak -proper language to use for your future? Look at the way you are dressed! This is not the way our fathers dressed. Go and change now!

[The mother freezes]

Narrator: See, what Mum is really trying to say this time is, 'Treat me with respect and I'll do the same, ' and also, 'You always try to be someone else, but just be yourself because I love you the way you are.

Mum: Go!

Boy 2: Bye Ma, see you ….

The mother continues cleaning but then a girl comes into the house. She throws her school bag, her books and her shoes around the house as she walks. The mother is shocked.

Mum: Wow! Let me see. What are you doing? You make a mess and I clean it up! Come and tidy up. I get up early in the morning. I clean the house -even your room. I cook for you. I wash the dishes. I wash your clothes. I feed the baby. Aahh!! *[screaming]*.

Girl: Clean my room Mum.

Mum: You go and clean it now and also clean up the mess you've made. I have so many things to do right now. *[The mother freezes]*

Narrator: Oh! What mum really wants to say here is, 'Mmm, the condition of your room is a reflection on who you are or what your life is like. A clean and tidy room reflects the way we behave and a tidy room makes us feel comfortable and relaxed.'

[another young girl comes into the house with a lot of books and a school bag. She's holding a big certificate with a B grade written on it]

Girl: Mum ... Mum!

Mum : What ... ?

Girl: *[happily]* Look what I've got!

Mum: What? B grade! My dear, I'm so proud of you!
[a great hug between them. Freeze]

Narrator: What mum is really trying to say now is, 'D or B I'm so proud of you.' Yes, that's right. Sometimes mum does what it's right to do. Mum is always proud of you not just for your performance but because of who you are. So, you see, mothers are complex because they're created by God. They love us all and sometimes they are funny in the way they express how much they care. They use various ways to convey the same message. Sometimes Mums feed you yucky vegetables, they stop you from watching TV, they expect you to be perfect in your studying, force you to sweep the floor. But in the end what we want to say whether mum is right or wrong is 'I love you!'

Everyone: We love you too Mum!

● ● ●

Pottery and Rain

This play was created and performed by Doha Hmoud, Marwa Ahmad, Safa Ahmad, Dalia Suliman and Salam from Fatima Al-Zahra secondary girls school, Jerusalem Suburbs, Palestine with support from their teacher Sarah Zahran. A recording of the play performed by the actors is available here...

https://youtu.be/Ri3W-q1TPdo

Narrator: Once upon a time there was a man from Jenin city in Palestine; he had two daughters; the first daughter married a young man from Jalameh village; the second one married a young man from Geba village. One day, the father wanted to check that his daughters were OK, so he rode on his donkey to the first married daughter's house in Jalameh village.

Father: Hi my darling. How are you? How are your children and your husband?

The daughter: It hasn't been raining all year and we fear drought and hunger, so we pray to God day and night to bring rain because my children are still young. The oldest one is just eight years old.

Father: Don't worry. Don't worry, our God will help you and it will rain.

The daughter: I hope so. I really hope so. May God help us.

Narrator: The father returned to his home in Jenin. Two weeks later it rained for two weeks. The father rejoiced for his daughter. Then he decided to visit his second daughter in Geba.

Father: Hi my daughter, How are you? How are your children and your husband?

The daughter: Unfortunately, we live in very difficult conditions because we made lots of pots two weeks ago and they still haven't dried because of the heavy rain. We always pray to God to stop the rain so that the pottery will dry and we can sell it.

Father: Don't worry. Don't worry my daughter. Our God will help you and your children.

The daughter: May God help us. Please help us.

Narrator: When the father returned to his home, his wife asked him:

Mother: Tell me, how are our daughters?

Father: If it rains, your daughter and her children in Geba will die of hunger. If it stops raining, your daughter in Jalameh and her children will die of hunger.

Narrator: As the old saying says: Parents will be responsible for their daughters until they die.

[hum albanat lilamamaat هم البنات للممات]

● ● ●

Sarah says...
"Pottery and rain is a very old, traditional story which comes from Palestinian culture. I read the text with the students and we summarized it and translated it into English. We then discussed the setting and the necessary props to perform it. After intensive training, my students did a great job of performing it. I think they benefitted a lot from discussing the morals and what else can be learnt from it. Their English language level and their self-confidence improved a lot by memorising the script and performing the play."

The Fighter

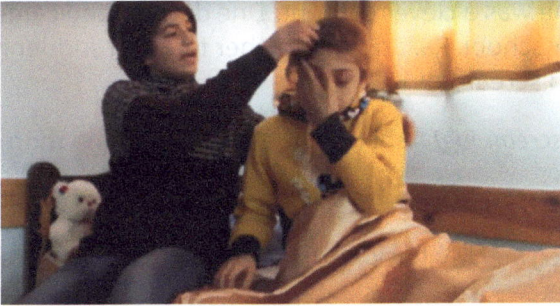

This play was created and performed by Roqaya Shabat, Sara Rizq Al Zaanin, Sara Ahmed Al Zaanin, Maha Al–Athamna, and Rawan Al-Zaanin from Beit Hanoun Elementary Co-ed UNRWA school, Gaza with support from their teacher Sahar Salha. A recording of the actors performing the play is available here...

https://youtu.be/zQWYxW7gvBg

[In Razan's bedroom]

Dad : Razan, Razan . Good morning my daughter.

Razan : Good morning, dad!

Dad: Wake up my daughter. It's school time. It's a new year. You became a third grader.

Narrator : Once upon a time, there was a beautiful girl called Razan. She was a clever student. One day her dad came to wake her up for school. Razan stood on her feet and suddenly, she fell down and screamed

Razan : *[screaming]* Aah! Help me mum! Help me mum!

Mum : What happened to you Razan? Why did you fall down?

Razan : *[crying]* My back hurts. I have a headache. I can't stand on my feet .

Mum : Ok, go to sleep now and tomorrow you can go to school.

Narrator : Mum told dad what happened with Razan

Dad : Tomorrow I will take her to the doctor after school to examine her. Don't worry! She will be ok.

Mum : OK I hope so *[looking to the heavens]*

Narrator : The next morning, Razan went to school. During break time, she fell down and the headmaster called her parents. Dad took Razan to the doctor and told him what happened with his daughter.

Doctor : *[At the clinic]* Hello

Dad : Hello, doctor

Doctor : Have a seat.

Dad : Thank you!

Doctor : What's the matter?

Dad : My daughter has a headache and she can't stand on her feet .

Doctor : Don't worry. She will be healthy.

Narrator : The doctor started to examine her and seemed very sad.

Doctor : Sorry to tell you , your daughter has blood cancer.

Dad : Oh my God! I can't believe it!

Doctor : And she must go to Bethlehem soon to start her treatment.

Narrator : Dad returned home very sad and he didn't want to tell mum because she suffers from heart disease.

Mum : What's the matter?

Dad : Nothing.

Mum : What's wrong with my daughter?

Dad : Nothing.

Mum : But you look very sad.

Dad : *[sadly]* My daughter has blood cancer.

Mum : No, no. I won' t lose Razan. Razan will live.

Dad : And she must go to Bethlehem to start her medicine.

Mum :I will be with her.

Dad : You can't go with her.

Mum : But I must be with her. She's my soul, she's my life, she's my heart.

Narrator : Razan went to Bethlehem and she had her chemical doses.

Doctor : Hello, Razan.

Razan : Hello, doctor.

Doctor : Don't worry. You will be ok. Mashallah, Mashallah

Narrator : Razan sends her videos to mum.

Razan : *[recording a video]* Hello mum. Hello dad. Hello teachers. Hello friends. I miss you so much. This is from Razan. *[kissing]* Look, I'm studying. This is my English book. I need your prayers to get better.

Narrator : Razan needs your prayers. Pray for Razan.

●　●　●

Sahar says..
"Despite being in the era of global communication, Palestinian children still suffer from the siege, from poverty and many other problems. So they really appreciated having the chance to convey messages to the world about love, peace, hope, dreams, illness, siege, poverty, war and social problems that the Hands Up Project gave them through the playwriting competition.

My students and I had a great experience preparing for the competition but choosing the topic for the play was really difficult. We discussed different ideas a lot and eventually decided to focus on a real story about a student in our school who suffers from cancer.

I'm so pleased that the girls worked really well as a team in writing the script in Arabic. They then individually translated it into English. When everyone had their own translation they all worked together again to produce the best English version they could. It was nice to see them using the internet to look up words and expressions to use in their play. They then discussed a suitable location to film it, the costumes, props, and background music, and then chose people to be the actors. In the end they produced something pure of their own which made them feel more confident.

In short, the process of creating our plays inspires the girls and the teachers to produce their own literature not just for competitions, but also for life. When a twelve year old student has her or his own literature published in a book, this means that the Hands Up Project opens the space for Palestinian kids to become their own Shakespeares. Here is what some of the actors said about the experience of creating our play "The fighter":

Roqaya , the narrator
"This drama means that we can write and act . I'm happy because we are little actors"

Sara , the doctor
"My dream in life is to be a doctor and I'm happy that I played this role in the play. When I join such activities, I feel that I am distinguished"

Rawan ,the patient
"I become more confident when I participated in this activity. I want to do more in the future. There is nothing impossible with my teacher –Sahar – and my parents' support."

Maha , the mum
"I'm not afraid to speak English anymore. I will be on Youtube . I'm a star!"

Sara, the dad
"Engaging in such activity helps to practice my hobby and speak English and transfers our ideas and feelings to the world"

Sa'sa' and Ma'ma'

This play was created and performed by Ihda Abu Khiran, Raghad Moqbel, Banan Samahin, Raneem Ghwanmeh, and Lilian Nofe from Arroub Basic Girls School, Hebron, Occupied Palestine with support from their teacher Intisar Jawabreh Jawabreh.
A recording of the play, performed by the actors can be seen here...

https://youtu.be/UAxRbf4fDLU

Narrator: Once upon a time there was a goat and her two babies, Ma'ma' and Sa'sa'. They lived in a cottage up in the mountains. The mother went to the fields every day to bring them food and they stayed at home, waiting.

Mother: Babies, I want to go now. I will bring you milk and grass. Don't open the door to anybody but me. Be careful! I saw the wolf watching our house. Perhaps he is trying to get in. Be careful and stay calm till I come back.

Sa'sa': Goodbye.

Ma'ma': Take care.

Narrator: A little while later the wolf arrived at the house.

Wolf: *[outside the door, chanting]* Hey Sa'sa'! Hey Ma'ma'. I am your mother. My hands are full of grass. My breasts are full of milk. Open the door babies.

Sa'sa': Oh! Mum has come, Ma'ma'! Mum has come. Let's open the door.

Ma'ma': No - don't open the door! This is the wolf. Just wait. You are not our mother. Your voice is harsh , but my mother's voice is soft. You are the wolf. Go from here right now

Wolf: Okay, I will go, but I will find a way to get you!

Narrator: The wolf went to the drugstore, and he bought a solution to make his voice soft.

Wolf: I will drink this solution now and my voice will be soft. *[outside the door again, chanting in a softer voice]* Hey Sa'sa'! Hey Ma'ma'. I am your mother. My hands are full of grass. My breasts are full of milk. Open the door babies.

Sa'sa': This is our mother's song, and her voice as well. Let's open the door right now.

Ma'ma': Wait sister! Let's make sure. Mum would you please show us your finger.

Wolf: My finger? Why?

Ma'ma': Put it up to the glass please.

Wolf: Okay, here is my finger.

Ma'ma': No, you are not our mother. You are the wolf! Mum's fingers are white and yours are black. Go from here damned wolf! We will tell mother. She will kill you!

Narrator: The wolf went to the miller, and he bought a bag full of flour. He tipped it over his body, and he became white. Then he went to the goat's house.

Wolf: [outside the door again, chanting] Hey Sa'sa'! Hey Ma'ma'. I am your mother. My hands are full of grass. My breasts are full of milk. Open the door babies.

Sa'sa': Mum has come back! Mum has come. Mum show us your hand.

Narrator: The wolf showed his finger and they opened the door. The wolf suddenly attacked and the baby goats started running. He caught Ma'ma' but Sa'sa' managed to hide. When the wolf was full he drank a bottle of water, and went to sleep under the tree.

Wolf: What a big meal! I feel sleepy now. A nap is the right thing to do.

Narrator: The mother came back after a long day in the fields. Her hands were full of grass and her breasts were full of milk and she started singing.

Mother: Hey Sa'sa'! Hey Ma'ma'. I am your mother. My hands are full of grass. My breasts are full of milk. Open the door babies. But the door is open! Where are you babies? Sa'sa'! Ma'ma'! Where are you?

Sa'sa': Mum! Mum! The nasty wolf cheated us. He made himself into you Mum.

Mum: Ma'ma', your sister? He ate her? Tell me.

Sa'sa': He did mum!

Mother: Come on, let's move quickly.

Narrator: The mother goat saw the wolf lying in the shade, snoring. He was full and his tummy was so big. The mother attacked him, and opened up his tummy. She took Ma'ma' out.

Mother: This lesson shouldn't be forgotten. From now on, you have to be more careful!

● ● ●

Intisar says..
"The story of Sa'sa' and Ma'ma' is from Palestinian heritage. My Grandma used to tell it to us as a bedtime story and my Mum did the same with my children. In our version we made the language as simple as we could to suit the level of the students, but it was quite easy for them anyway since they are familiar with the story. I faced some difficulties to train them in acting because I lack the skills in that myself but we tried our best and the children were very enthusiastic about having the chance to win and travel to London. They worked really hard and I think it was a nice experience for them to act and express their emotions through drama. Even though they didn't win the competition they were really proud about having their play published on Youtube. Thanks to the Hands Up Project for the opportunities you provide to our students."

Unity Play

This play was created and performed by Dana Nawas, Rawan El Bahnasawi, Batool Mohsen, Nada El Khatib, and Raghad El Na'ami from Nuseirat Prep [A] Girls UNRWA school, Gaza with support from their teacher Mariam Abu Seifan. A recording of the actors performing the play is available at

https://youtu.be/NCnzCFOetW0

Narrator: Once upon a time there was a very happy family. The family consisted of three members: a widow and two sons: Ahmed and Ali. After the death of the father, mum took the full responsibility. She did her best and succeeded in keeping her family happy. But, what happened? Let's see.

Scene 1
[The mother and two sons are working on the land]

Ahmed : Good job my dear brother.

Ali : Thank you. Let's have a rest after a long busy day.

Ahmed : My brother, I think we should sow a new crop tomorrow.

Ali: I agree with you. We should start right after sunrise.

Ahmed : Deal! *[Shaking hands]*

Mother : Oh my beloved children. I'm so proud of you. God bless you.

Scene 2
[Ali is working on the land]

Devil: You paid more effort than your brother. You can make your own decisions.

Ali: Yes, yes! I can make my own decisions.

Ahmed: My brother, let's go and sow wheat.

Ali: No, corn is better.

Ahmed: Wheat is better, and it's very suitable for our land this year.

Ali: Corn is better, corn is better!

Devil: Don't listen. Your choice is the best.

Ali: My choice is the best. Corn is better. Corn is better.

Mum: Calm down, calm down my son. Let's sow wheat.

Devil: See! She loves him more than you.

Ali: You love him more than me.

Mom: Oh, my son! You're both my dearest sons. I love you both. *[Ali laughs sarcastically]*

Devil: Divide the land

Ali: Let's divide the land.

Ahmed: Oh no!

Mother: Division?! Division?! No! That's impossible! Division? No! No! *[A fence appears]*

Scene 3

Ali: I'm very tired, I'm very tired little crops. Oh, my God!

Devil: Everything will be ok, work alone.

Ali: It's better to be away from them.

Ahmed: I'm very tired. I'm very tired, little crops. I wish I could work with my brother again. I wish I could get rid of this crazy fence. Oh, my God! Help us! Help us for our mother's sake!

Devil: You always think of your brother but he doesn't think of you at all. His part is bigger than yours. You can't even take your rights. Weak boy!

Ahmed: No, I'm not weak. I can do it. *[Ahmed goes to his brother's part.]*

Ahmed: Hey! Hey, your part is bigger than mine.

Ali: What?!

Ahmed: The two parts should be equal. I should take from your part and add it to mine.

Ali: Are you dreaming?! Stop it!

Ahmed: No, I won't!

[Mum collapses]

Ali and Ahmed: Mum, mum! We're so sorry. Forgive us. Wake up, mum!

Mother: Are you together again?

Ali and Ahmed: Yes, yes. We're together.

Mother: Thank God. *[They get rid of the fence]*

Mum: My advice to you, my children, is unity. Be together whatever happens, work together, sow together and you will reap together.

Mum and the two sons, hand in hand: Unity, unity, unity! Stop division!

Narrator: Let's stand hand in hand. *[The two sons, the mother and the narrator sing a song]* Let's stand hand in hand, raise your voice and say we're one, let's stay side by side, we'll never lose but always win!

● ● ●

Mariam says..

How was the play created ?
"The idea of our play developed from the state of division we live in in Palestine. Palestinian children are greatly influenced by this division and it makes people quarrel with each other. This play reflects what we as Palestinians dream to have in reality. We want unity and peace. Palestinian children want to live happily and safely like other children around the world. We do believe that our dream will come true one day."

How did the students benefit from the experience?

Dana Nawas
"When Mrs. Mariam told us about the competition, I became very motivated. I had the idea of the play and started to write. I wrote many drafts. I learned many new English words. I used the dictionary; I asked my teacher. It was an amazing experience to write a play in English. This is my real start in writing".

Rawan El Bahnasawi
"This experience gave me more self-confidence. I got rid of my shyness and fear. I am now able to stand in front of people to speak and express myself. It is a big change in my character, I think."

Batool Mohsen
"I love acting. This play helped to acquire many important skills in acting and communication. It helped me to feel and live what I act. Really, it's amazing to impress people by your performance."

Nada El Khatib
"Although I acted the devil character, I was happy to do that. I was very satisfied at the end when I was kicked out of the happy family's life because this showed the strong message of unity versus division in a very simple and convincing way. Also, I developed my linguistic skills in English."

Raghad El Na'ami
"This experience taught me many important lessons. I learned how to develop my skills. I learned that the more you train, the more skilful you'll be. Also, you keep trying and trying to give the best you can. This put me in challenge with myself to give the best. Working in a team was amazing. I made 4 more friends."

My Mother-in-Law Is a Trouble Maker

This play was created and performed by Nour Salam, Amani al Buhaisi, Nagham Abu Rabee, Shahd Abu Amra, and Manar Abu Zeita from Deir al Balah Prep [A] girls UNRWA school, Gaza with the support of their teacher Camellia H Salem. A recording of the play performed by the actors is available here..

https://youtu.be/0R-pPzK4Q8U

Narrator: One morning the mother-in-law asked her daughter-in-law to prepare tea.

Mother-in-law: Idiot!

Daughter-in-law: What did you say?

Mother-in-law: Oh, my sweet daughter-in-law.

Daughter-in-law: Yes, mother-in-law

Mother-in-law: Is the tea ready?

Daughter-in-law: Five more minutes

Mother-in-law: Oh, such a lazy person she is!

Daughter-in-law: *[aside]* I hope you burn in hell.

Narrator: An hour later the daughter-in-law is sweeping the floor.

Mother-in-law: Clean this place better, clean it well.

Daughter-in-law: I did clean it. Are you blind? Can't you see? I just cleaned it! I cleaned it lots of time, can't you see?

Mother-in-law: You are blind, look it's not clean!

Daughter-in-law: I am blind that I came to this house!

Mother-in-law: I'm blind that I let you into this house!

Daughter-in-law: Are you disabled, that you are making me clean. Can't you do it yourself?

Mother-in-law: Don't talk back!

Daughter-in-law: I learned it from you

In the afternoon

Mother-in-law: Where is the food? You are very lazy.

Daughter-in-law: Here you are.

Mother-in-law: Why are you so late with the food?

Daughter-in-law: I was making the food for you. That's why I'm late

Mother-in-law: Let me taste it. What's this? What kind of food is this?

Daughter-in-law: I learned it from you.

Mother-in-law: I cook this bad food, huh?

Daughter-in-law: Yeah! You showed me how to cook this food.

Mother-in-law: I cook like this? You are such an idiot!

Daughter-in-law: I learned it from you as well. If you don't like it, don't eat it. I will take it. Go cook for yourself.

Mother-in-law: Just wait until my son comes home!

Daughter-in-law: I will let him know too!

Narrator: There is a knock at the door

Daughter-in-law: Welcome my friend. Come in.

The guest: How are you darling?

Daughter-in-law: Actually, I'm so sad

The guest: Why?

Daughter-in-law: My mother-in-law always drives me crazy.

The guest: I'll take you to a wise man who can help you.

Narrator: The two ladies leave the house.

Daughter-in-law: Good evening, sir. I love my mother-in-law but she hates me.

The wise man: Take this bottle of poison. Add 3 drops in her tea every day. In a month she will die secretly. But remember, you will do the mission yourself.

Narrator: Next morning...

Daughter-in-law: Good morning mum. I got up early to prepare your tea on time.

Mother-in-law: God bless you daughter!

Narrator: Day by day things became better between them. Love and warmth strengthened the relationship. The guest visited her again on the last day

Daughter-in-law: *[crying]* I love her please help me I don't want her to die!

Narrator: They go back to the wise man.

Daughter-in-law: I want her alive please help me ..I love her ..I can't live without her!

The wise man: Dear! Listen... I gave you a bottle of water!

Mother-in-law: Oh, thank God!

● ● ●

Camellia says...
"In Palestine we have lots of proverbs related to our mothers-in-law and most of them aren't positive! Some examples are 'A boat full of sisters-in-law can go quickly but a boat full of mothers-in-law won't move at all' and 'On the gates of Paradise it is written that a mother-in-law will never love her daughter-in-law' and 'Satan will enter Paradise before a mother-in-law loves her daughter-in-law' We accepted the challenge to write a play for the Hands Up Project playwriting competition but wanted to create something using a story that is much more positive than these proverbs. I helped my students write the scenario and then they started to work on the characters and the performance. In this play we found a way to mend the relationship between them by building friendship. The message here is that we might only realise that we care about somebody when we think we are going to lose them."

The Golden Lira

This play was created and performed by Mena el Ghora, Sahar Nashwan, Nadia EL Saqqa, and Bareaa El Wehaidy from Zaitoun Prep [B] girls UNRWA school, Gaza with support from their teachers Weam Abdel Bari and Nisreen Hammad. A recording of the play, performed by the actors is available here...

https://youtu.be/-xNZl6uWbZo

Narrator: In a big and beautiful village there was an old rich man. He had a son called Ibrahim who wasn't like his father. He was very lazy and depended, to a large extent, on his father's wealth. The old man was angry and worried; he wanted his son to be a man.

The old man: My son, you should work hard to earn money. You must be a man.

Ibrahim: Why should I?

The old man: *[angrily]* But you should depend on yourself! You're not a little baby anymore. Now get out and don't return until you have earned a golden lira.

Ibrahim: *[angrily]* Ok, dad.

Narrator: The next morning the son was walking towards the door and his mother stopped him.

The mother: Ibrahim, my son.

Ibrahim: Yes, mum.

The mother: Listen, take this. It's a golden lira. Go out and come back after two hours. Tell your father that you have earned this lira from your work.

Ibrahim: Ok, mum. Thank you very much.

Narrator: The son did what his mother had told him and he came back with the golden lira.

Ibrahim: *[happily]* Dad , dad! I have worked for two hours to earn this lira .

The old man: This is not the one I want. Go and bring another one. *[he throws the lira in the fire]*

Narrator: The next morning Ibrahim was walking towards the door again and again his mother stopped him.

The mother: Ibrahim, take this golden lira and don't come back until three days have passed so that your father will believe you.

Ibrahim: Ok, mum.

Narrator: After three days Ibrahim came back again with the golden lira.

Ibrahim: Dad, dad look I have worked hard for three days to earn this lira.

The old man: This is not the one I want. Go and bring another one [throwing the golden lira in the fire again]

Ibrahim: [angrily] Ok dad. Bring ... bring...... bring .... bring .... Why? ...... Why?

Narrator: The next morning Ibrahim left early while his mother was sleeping. He worked hard for a month and he earned a golden lira. When he came back...

Ibrahim: Dad, look I swear I have worked hard for a month to earn this.

The old man: This is not the one I want. Go and bring another one. [He tried to throw the lira in the fire but Ibrahim prevented him]

Ibrahim: You can't do this! I really worked hard to earn this golden lira.

Narrator: The old man smiled and hugged his son.

The old man: Now you're a man my son. The previous times you didn't get angry when I threw the lira in the fire because you didn't work hard to have it. Easy come, easy go!

Narrator: Now what do you understand from our story?

●　●　●

Weam says....
"The Golden Lira is a traditional Palestinian story that deals with the concept of self-confidence and self-worth; a matter that emerges via the relationship between the boy [Ibrahim] and his father. The students of The Hands Up Project were extremely motivated to act out the play and they were chosen according to their acting abilities and to what extent each student found the character close to her own personality."

47

Live Your Life

This play was created and performed by Shaza Hamad, Sally Hweihi, Razan Hweihi, Marwa Hamad, and Malak Hamdan from Beit Hanoun prep girls UNRWA school [A], Gaza, with support from their teachers, Manal Ismail and Rinan Al Mazanin. A recording of the play being performed by the actors is available here...

https://youtu.be/PeofGSQet3I

Grandpa: [Grandpa enters the stage] Life is sweet. I have lived my life in every single detail. Though I'm getting older, I'm still strong enough to go on. I still have my teeth, healthy, healthy! [Parents enter the stage carrying a carpet with a big calendar written on it. The mother steps on the different dates as she speaks]

Mum: Come on Abou-Mahmoud, hurry up! Listen Abou-Mahmoud, I'm worried about our daughters' future. I want the years to pass fast. This year, I want them to get married and this year, I want them to have babies. Oh and this year, I'll feel relieved and free from responsibilities.

Dad: That's true dear! Girls are a heavy burden. What should we do?

Grandpa: [talking to the parents] That's nonsense. Let the girls live their lives normally!

[Parents leave and girl 1 enters the stage]

Girl 1: Hello, grandpa! [gives him a kiss]

Grandpa: Hi, sweetie! Have you finished your book?

Girl 1: Sure! Imagine grandpa! I dream of the day in which I get the first rank in the reading competition. All social media will talk about me. I'll be famous. I love reading books. It's my favourite hobby.

Girl 2: [Girl 2 enters the stage talking to Grandpa] Oh! But I have a different dream. I want to be a famous designer. I like making clothes and designs. I promise you Grandpa that you'll wear my first design. It'll be a fabulous suit.

Grandpa: [Grandpa talks to granddaughters] I'm sure of that honey. I'm so proud of you.

Mum: [The parents enters the stage. Mum talks to the girls] Take off the glasses and the books, the scissors and the clothes - throw them away! [talking to girl 1] Come here, Look at me. You wear glasses. You won't marry. What will people say? You have a defect. No one will marry you. Forget about reading, think of yourself as a beautiful bride. *[talking to girl 2]* And you , take these high-heeled shoes. You'll look taller and prettier like a lady. This will bring you more handsome grooms. Oh God! How can I overcome these problems? One wears glasses and the other is too short.

Dad: *[talking to Mum]* Easy, easy dear! Everything will be all right. Calm down.

Grandpa: *[talking to the whole family]* Come here my son. Your daughters are gracious and kind but they need to live their own lives. Every girl has her own dream and she enjoys her life as it is. Don't push them too soon or too hard. We are in two thousand and seventeen. We can't rush through the years. Take things slowly. And you granddaughters, don't let anyone destroy your dreams and your future. Live life happily and normally!

Both girls: *[standing side by side, chanting]* This is our life! We want to enjoy it. Please, don't pressure us! We love you parents.

● ● ●

Manal and Rinan say....
"We were filled with happiness and excitement when we heard the news of our winning the third place in the playwriting competition. But at the same time we weren't surprised since we know that our students have great skills and abilities. They were so enthusiastic about creating the play, and put everything of themselves into it as they enjoyed so much.

From doing this play, we realised how important drama is in revealing outer and inner feelings and expressing thoughts. As a result, we're now emphasising more and more the importance of using drama in teaching inside the classroom. It helps students to overcome some of their educational difficulties and to break the usual routine from traditional methods of teaching".

We asked Shatha, who played the role of the grandpa, about her experience. She said, "When we started writing the play, I wanted to make something that would challenge the idea of a male-dominated society in Palestine. I enjoyed playing a grandpa who was wise and more responsible, and who gave good advice and help"

Malak and Marwa, who played the father and the daughter roles, agreed about this. "We wanted to make a play about patience, and having the strength to defy all the obstacles to make our dreams come true"

Chapter 2

School

Education is very highly valued in Palestine and, since the writers of the plays submitted for the competition spend many hours of the week at school [six days a week in Gaza], it's hardly surprising that there were many plays about this topic. In **Child Labour** and **Stolen dreams!** we hear about two children who, for economic reasons, are not able to go to school. Of course, problems at home can have a direct impact on what happens in the classroom, and an example of this is portrayed in **The little girl's secret.** The common worldwide school issues of tribalism and bullying are explored in **Little Hypocrites** and **The Bullied**, and then in **Am I different?** a potential solution is offered to these problems. **Teddy and his teacher Miss Thompson** looks at the incredible power that teachers have to build children's confidence. The last play, **Us and them**, takes us out of the classroom, and shows how learning can happen through online link ups around the world.

Child Labour

This play was created and performed by Shatha Takkona, Dalya Abu Tabaq, Sara Zomlot, and Baraa Al Maqousi from Halab elementary Co-ed [B] school, Gaza with support from their teachers, Jamela Mohammed, Sahar Salha and Heba Ziyad. A recording of the play, performed by the actors is available here...

https://youtu.be/r9V_w9cwQyQ

Scene. A busy street at rush hour in the afternoon. A brother and sister are sitting in the back seat of a car, on their way to the afternoon shift at school. The car is stuck at a red light. Imad starts cleaning the car windows.

Imad: *[singing while cleaning the windows of a car]* I clean the car to be beautiful, I polish the glass to see the life, beautiful.

Sara: *[sitting in the back seat of the car, frowning at the boy outside]* Look at this boy, he's not clean. Make him go away! *[Ahmed starts to open the window]* Close the window!!!

Ahmed: *[looking sadly at the boy]* Hey, come here. What's your name?

Imad: *[with a blank expression]* Imad

Ahmed: Why do you work? Don't you go to school?

Imad: *[answering sadly]* No, I left the school early when my father died.

Ahmed: Don't you like learning?

Imad: *[talking to himself]* Don't like to learn? *[staring at Ahmed's book]* Who doesn't like to learn?! *[He drops his cloth]* But how can I and my family live and eat? *[staring at Sara's apple]* Food.....learning.......food........learning *[putting his hands on his head]* Oh, my God!

Ahmad: Answer me please, Imad?

Imad: *[sadly]* You have food, education, and dad but, for me I don't.

Ahmad: Do you know the alphabet?

Imad: A little bit.

Ahmad: I have an idea! *[Imad looks at Ahmad eagerly to know what the idea is]* I come to school every day by this road, so I can help you. Take these words to remember them *[Ahmad gives Imad a piece of paper]*, then I will give you new words to learn each day.

Imad: Thank you very much. So, I can work and learn at the same time. *[The lights change to green]*

Ahmad: *[closing the window of the car]* See you!

Imad: *[picking up the cloth with one hand and waving it, and with the other holding the paper to his chest]* Goodbye.

●   ●   ●

Jamela says...
"I told the students about the Hands up Project competition and encouraged them to think about a play to be acted by them at our school. Two days later some of my students told me a story about a poor boy they always see near our school who cleans and polishes cars every day in heavy traffic to save money and help his big family. The whole class found this very moving so we decided to work on this story and act it as a play. By doing the play they improved in their acting skills, learnt some new words and felt freer to speak and express their feelings. But above all this the play made them think about how they can help people who are even less fortunate than themselves."

Stolen Dreams!

This play was created and performed by Zeina Abu Zeid, Aya Zahran, Judy Eid, Lyan Aldorbashy, and Farah Thabet from Al Rimal Prep 'A' school, Gaza with support from their teacher, Fatma Al Jarrah. A recording of the play, performed by the actors is available here..

https://youtu.be/fAHGyGdyMAU

Scene 1. Zeina is a little girl in 6th grade. Her mother died when she was 6 years old. Zeina is the oldest amongst her sisters and brothers. She has 3 brothers and 3 sisters; all are younger than her. After her mother died, she has to take care of her little siblings. Zeina is an excellent student. She loves school and thinks of it as her refuge. But Zeina has to balance being a student and being a substitute mum for her siblings. Zeina's father is always angry. He is always shouting and always accusing Zeina of not helping enough. The scene opens as Zeina is studying, sitting on the floor. Her dad comes in shouting.

Dad: *[tearing away her books and shouting]* Hey! What are you doing? I told you I don't want you to go to school!

Zeina: But dad! I love school! I love school!

Dad: I said no school! Go take care of your brothers! They're dirty and hungry! I am hungry too! Go make us food! School! Ha! No school from now on!

Zeina: *[crying]*: But dad, please! I beg you! *[she grabs his legs]*

Dad: Go now! Make us food!

Zeina: *[crying]* ok!!!

Scene 2. The scene opens with Zeina holding her mum's picture and weeping

Zeina: *[crying heavily]*: Mum!! I miss you, mum! Why did you go? I need you!! Please come back! I can't take it anymore! Life is so hard!! My dad wants to deprive me from school. He wants me to babysit my brothers and sisters! Please, come back!!! We need you!

Scene 3. The scene opens with Zeina sitting with her friends: Layan, Judy and Farah..

The four friends are sitting and chatting. Zeina looks the saddest.

Friends: What's wrong, Zeina? Why are you sad?

Zeina *[sadly]*: My dad wants me to stop coming to school. He wants me to babysit my brothers and sisters!

Friends: Noooooooooooooooo!

Zeina: I love school! I want to go to school! I want to learn! I want to be with my friends! I have dreams like anyone else!

Layan: I know how hard it is to lose a mum and be the oldest.

Judy: I know the pain of losing a parent.. I lost my dad in the last war.. and I know exactly the pain you're feeling!

Farah: I am so sorry, Zeina. But you're such a strong girl. You are a mum and you're only 11 years old. You're excellent at school! You can't stop coming to school! We'll go to talk to your dad. Don't worry!

Friends: Yes! We'll go and talk to him.

Layan: But remember! We are all here for you! So wipe away your tears! Smile..

Zeina: *[smiling]* Thank you for being here with me. I love you so much.

Farah: And now let's talk about our dreams! Zeina, what would you like to do?

Zeina: Fly.. I want to fly!!

Friends: Then! Let's help her fly. *[The friends pick Zeina up and make her fly. Everyone laughs out loud and eventually they put Zeina down]*

Judy: Yes! That's the spirit, Zeina! You have to always remember...It doesn't matter how big our dreams are, we can always make it happen. Keep dreaming and keep doing the things you love.

[The scene ends with friends giggling, laughing, hugging and singing...]

The Little Girl's Secret

This play was written as a story in Arabic by Zina Abd Alkareem Alsosi, a 4th grade pupil at Jabalia UNRWA Elementary Co-ed School [D], Gaza. It was then converted into English and into a play by her teacher Ihsan Samih Udwan, and then performed by Zina and her classmates. A recording of the play, performed by the actors is available here...

https://youtu.be/2EteZJL3Va8

Scene one. The teacher comes in, greets the class and starts writing on the blackboard the subject, the day and the date.

Teacher: Good morning children.

All students: Good morning Miss Iman.

Teacher: How are you?

All students: Fine thanks. What about you?

Teacher: Fine too thank you. Sit down. *[She starts to explain the lesson when suddenly...]*

Nagham: *[standing up]* Miss, can I go to the bathroom, please.

Teacher: Sure you can, but don't be late. *[When Nagham came back after a while she asked again]*

Nagham: Please Miss, I need to go again.

Teacher: Ok, but this is the last time.

Nagham: *[Shortly afterwards]* Miss, Miss I want to go now to the bathroom, please Miss Iman.

Teacher: *[surprised]* What's wrong with you Nagham?! OK go!

The bell rings and the class ends. Miss Iman takes Nagham with her to the head teacher to tell her what happened.

Head teacher : Why do you go to the bathroom a lot. Are you OK? Should I call the doctor?

Nagham: *[crying]* No, No! I need my mum.

Teacher: Ok, we will call her. Don't worry.

Scene 2. In Nagham's mother's house. The mother is boiling water and her three children are crying around her, hungry. There is no food to eat, only boiled water.

Mum: Ok don't cry my kids. The food will be ready soon. Just drink some water and you will be ok.

The phone rings.

Head teacher: Hello, This is Nagham's school. Are you her mother?

Mum: Yes, what's happened to my child?

Head teacher: Nothing. Don't worry. But we want you to come soon.

Mum: Ok I'll come straight away, bye.

The mother and her kids arrive at the school.

Head teacher: We want to be sure that Nagham is OK?

Mum : Yes she's well.

Headteacher: So, why does she go so much to the bathroom?

Mum: *[crying]* We are so poor. We have nothing to eat so..

Nagham: *[interrupting]* Don't tell my secret mum!

Mum: *[continuing]* She drinks so much water to fill her stomach - not to feel hungry.

Headteacher: Oh, I'm sorry. *[giving her some money]* Take Nagham with you and buy some food.

Mother: *[crying]* I need my children to live like other children live around the world.

● ● ●

Ihsan says...
This story was about a real pupil who used to go to the bathroom a lot. I met his mum and when I asked her if her kid was suffering from any disease she started crying and told me that they are so poor and there wasn't enough food to feed her children. So, their kids were forced to drink so much water to not feel hunger. Zina

decided to write about this story but to avoid causing any embarrassment she changed all the names. I helped her translate her story into English and then we decided to act it. My students felt so confident after acting in this play. I encouraged the writer, Zina to play the role of the mother. At the beginning she felt shy and refused because she is visually impaired, but in the end she played the role perfectly. I'm really proud of my strong and brilliant students.'

Little Hypocrites

This play was created and performed by May Ghazawneh, Nisreen kaabneh, Aya al-Lahaleeh and Siba Jaradat, from Alram girls secondary school, Palestine with support from their teacher Thaana Jamal Allen. A recording of the play performed by the actors is available here....

https://youtu.be/zNwBySgGGtk

Scene. Three friends are sitting gossiping at one side of the school playground [Nisreen, Aya and Mai]. On the other side of the playground, Siba is talking to their teacher. Suddenly Siba jumps up excitedly and hugs the teacher. The other girls watch this happening.

Mai: Oh my God did you see that? She looks so ugly!

Nisreen: Yes, her dress is so ugly.

Aya: Look out, she's coming.

Siba: *[running over to them excitedly]* Giiiirrrrlllllsssss!! Congratulate me. I'm going to be awarded the prize for the most distinguished student in the whole of Palestine. Can you believe it?

Nisreen: Nope ! Mmmm, I mean yeeessss of course.

Mai: I feel like I'm going to cry, I'm so happy for you!

Aya: Me too.

Siba: How lucky I am! I have the best friends in the whole world. I'm going to talk to the headmistress about it. *[All girls do a hi-five with their hands. Siba rushes off to go to the headmistress' office]*

Nisreen: Don't tell me that you really meant what you said?

Mai: Of course not! I don't understand why the teacher picked her.

Aya: There are many girls who deserve it more than her. You know what? It could be a mistake. It could be..

Mai: *[interrupting]* Yesssss ! It could be a mistake. It should be me. I'm going to ask the teacher about that and I'll be back.

Aya: I can't believe her! I didn't even finish. I was going to say it could be you.

Nisreen: She's so selfish!

Aya: And arrogant and mean

Nisreen: And horrible

Mai: *[suddenly coming back]* Who are you talking about?

Nisreen: Siba, of course! So...what happened?

Mai: This the worst day ever.

Aya: Why??

Mai: The teacher said that she deserves it. She's polite, active, smart .. bla, bla, bla..

Siba: *[coming back very excited from the headmistress' office]* Guess what !! The headmistress said that I can have one person to go with me. I really wish that I can pick you all, but I have just one choice.

Nisreen: Ohhhhh, it's not a big problem...

Mai: You can pick me!

Aya: Here she goes agaaaaain!

Nisreen: Excuse me!!!! Why you?

Mai: Because I'm her friend.

Nisreen: We are all her friends.

Aya: You said that there is a mistake and you deserve it more.

Siba: Whhaaaaat?!

Mai: Yes, but you also thought that earlier.

Nisreen: Ok, you made it easier! Now she can pick me.

Aya: Now, who is it who is selfish now? Let me think .. ..Oh, it's you!

Siba: What happened to you? I thought I had real friends but obviously I was totally wrong! You can trick some people sometimes, but not all the people all the time. I prefer to be alone than to have friends with two faces. *[she storms off]*

All: Two faces???!!

Mai: What's wrong with our faces? What does she mean?

Nisreen: I don't understand. I put make up on each morning.

Aya: Never mind! She thinks she is prettier than us! You are more beautiful than her.

Nisreen: You too. Till now I can't understand why they think she's clever?!

All: She's stupid! *[The bell rings]*

● ● ●

Thaana says...
"Frankly, I was initially hesitant about being part of the contest. Then I felt that if this is a ship, I must be the captain. I asked myself what is the worst thing that could happen? To lose? Then I remembered that the ship will never move or explore anything if I continue thinking like that. I met the girls and I told them this will be our game and we'll set its rules by writing and filming it. First, we started discussing the main idea and whether to write a comic or dramatic play. But then we preferred to write about something more realistic; Something the girls themselves live. The girls and I consider it as one of the most interesting experiences in our lives. We loved the idea of creating something and having the challenge of completing the whole job. Every morning these girls and others wait for me when I get to school and they ask me when they can do another play."

The Bullied

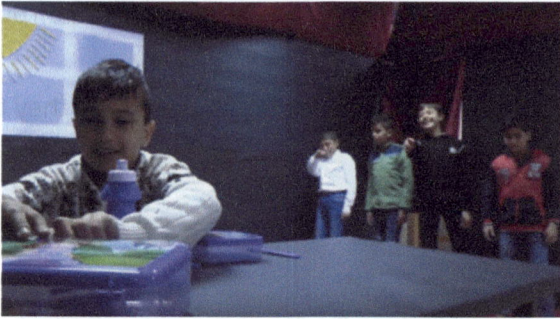

This play was created and performed by Mohannad Radwan, Ezzeddin Jaber, Naser Alhafi, Salah Aqel, and Hassan Alnairab from Palestine B UNRWA school, Jabalia, with support from their teacher, Imadeddin Almadhoun.

Scene. At the school canteen, at lunchtime. Four boys come into the canteen and see another boy getting ready to have his lunch sitting on a nice table by the window. Boy 2 approaches Boy 1 and slaps him from behind.

Boy 2: Give me your lunch you coward, and get away from this table.

Boy 1: Why did you do that? Leave me alone!

Boy 2: You are sitting at a nice table and I want it.

Boy 1: I was sitting here before you, so it's my place.

Boy 2: pushes Boy 1 again violently.

Boy 3: Yes, it's his table. You have no right to sit here. GET UP!

[Boy 4 and Boy 5 are standing near Boy 2, watching with an evil smile on their faces]

Boy 1: I will not leave here. This is my place. You cannot take it from me.

Boy 2: Yes, I can, and I will because I have them *[pointing at Boy 3, Boy 4 and Boy 5]*.

They pull Boy 1 away from the table and push him to the ground.

Boy 2: Get this coward away from my table! *[The others do what he asks with no questions]*

The lights go out. When the lights come up again Boy 2 is sitting at the table, eating Boy 1's lunch. Boy 3, 4 and 5 are protecting him while Boy 1 tries to get his place back. He is pushed to the ground every time. He does not give up and keeps trying.

Boy 1: *[talking to Boy 2's friends, on his knees]* It is not right. This is my place. You cannot give it to him.

Boy 3: It's his place now.

Boy 4: And it's his right to be here.

Boy 5: And you should find another place.

One is getting weaker and weaker every time he tries to get back to his place, he sits down hungry. He is under siege by Boy 2's friends in a tiny spot. Boy 1 and Boy 2 both stand up.

Boy 1: I will never give up and will keep trying until I get what is mine back.

Boy 2: *[laughing]* In your dreams you weak coward!

Boy 1: *[to Three, Four and Five]* Even if you protect him and make me hungry by stealing my food and you punish me for trying to have what is mine back, eventually things will return to their rightful owners.

Two and his friends laugh in an evil way.

Boy 3: He is stronger than you are. You should surrender.

Boy 4: Yeah, do as he says, and you will get to live.

Boy 1: NEVER!

The lights go out. When the lights come on again Boy 1 is standing right up close to the audience. He looks out in every direction. There is a very long pause. The lights go out. When the lights come on again Boy 1 is violently pushing Boy 3, Boy 4 and Boy 5. Darkness.

● ● ●

Imadeddin says...
"I only heard about the competition one week before the deadline and I wanted so much to participate, so I delivered the idea to my headmaster and he was of great support to my enthusiasm and facilitated everything for me. With the help of some of my colleagues I held auditions for students to choose the actors and within two days I found what I was looking for, so I met with the students and started to discuss ideas about the play until we reached an agreement about the theme. I asked the students for the events and they all discussed their ideas and we agreed on the events. That night I stayed up till around 4am, adjusting the final script based on their ideas. Then we made the set out of some unused furniture and black posters and curtains. One day before the deadline, we were ready to film the play. It was a very interesting challenge for us all."

Am I different?

This play was written and performed by Shahd Shalayel, Rinad Ismail Saja Joma'a, Rasha Abu Heen and Sammer Abu Arja from Zaytoun Prep [B] UNRWA school, Gaza with support from their teacher, Susan Musleh.

Saja: Hi! Have you ever felt different? Sometimes that's bad, sometimes it's good. It depends. Anyhow this is my story. It begins with my first day at my new school.

Teacher: Welcome your new classmate Saja! By the way, Saja is so clever. Her school report is excellent! Welcome Saja! I hope you enjoy your time in our school.

Saja: Thanks teacher.

Shahed: *[whispering]* Clever? Look at her clothes! Her shoes! Her glasses! She is so ugly.

Saja : Can I sit with you?

Sammer: What?!! You with us? Are you serious?

Saja: Yes please. I'd like to be your friend.

Shahed: You? With us? Friends? Look at yourself? Hahaha! You couldn't be our friend!

Saja: But why?

Sammer: Simply because you aren't like us. You're different. You're ugly. *[Sammar and Shahed leave]*

Saja arrives back at her home. She stares at the floor silently.

Mum: Hey Saja. You're home. How was your first day in your new school? Did you like it?

[Saja gives no answer.]

Mum : Saja! Saja ???? I am talking to you. *[Saja looks at her mum without speaking]* Saja, are you ok baby? Saja, answer me. You scare me! Are you ok baby?

Saja: *[exploding]* I am not going to this school again. I hate it. I hate people there and I hate myself *[crying]*

Mum: *[hugging Saja]* Hush now! Calm down baby, calm down. It's ok *[looking straight in Saja's eyes]*. Tell me what's going on baby?

Saja: Am I different mum? Am I ugly?

Mum: Ugly? Different? I don't understand.

Saja: The girls at school mocked me and rejected me. They said I'm different and ugly.

Mum : Of course you are different baby. You are polite, clever, friendly and cute. You are also so beautiful mashaallah!

Saja : Am I beautiful mum? Really?

Mum: Of course, baby you are so beautiful. In fact everyone is beautiful in his or her way. Do you know why?

Saja: Why mum?

Mum: Simply because Allah makes no mistakes. Saja, habibti, remember when we forgive others, we do a big favour to ourselves.

Saja: *[thinking for a while]* Allah makes no mistakes. You're right mum. I am beautiful and different in my way. *[smiling and hugging her mum]* Thanks Mum!

Mum : Any time, baby.

[a few days later]

Saja: Teacher, can I ask you a question please? Where is Shahed?

Teacher: Oh, Shahed has had an accident and she has to stay at home for two weeks.

Saja: Sammer

Sammer: What?

Saja: Do you mind visiting Shahed with me?

Sammer: You ? Shahed ?

Saja: Yes, please

Sammer: *[shocked]* Ok?!

At Shahed's house

Sammer: Look who is coming to see you?

Shahed: Who? *[very surprised]*

Saja: Hi Shahed. I'm sorry to hear about the accident. Don't worry about lessons. I will help you.

Shahed: You? Help me?

Sammer: Yes, she's very good at maths

Shahed : Ok *[pause]* Saja... I am sorry would you forgive me please?

Saja: Of course! We are friends, aren't we?

Shahed and Sammer: Of course.

Saja: *[to the audience]* You see.. to be different is the power. Why be something else?

You were born an original. Don't die a copy.

● ● ●

Susan says...
"Entering the playwriting competition was a marvellous experience. It gave my students a great opportunity to have fun. They also practised deep thinking and exchanging experiences through brain storming to gather ideas that reflect their feelings, thoughts, culture, concerns and ambitions. It was a chance for them to improve their debating skills through presenting their ideas for the play. In the end the work itself was the result of great teamwork to give birth to our play, which we are very proud of. Thanks a lot to everyone in the Hands Up Project. Your efforts are really appreciated by both teachers and students."

Teddy and His Teacher Miss Thompson

This play was created and performed by Haneen Abu Alkhair, Judy Dawood, Rahaf Almadhoon, Tarneem I'lyan and Ruba Almadhoon from Asma Prep girls UNRWA school A, Gaza with support from their teacher Saida Almadhoon. A recording of the play performed by the actors is available here...

https://youtu.be/q8VELoNlyL8

Teacher: *[in front of the class]* I love you all. I believe in your abilities. You are all creative and brilliant. *[aside]* I think Teddy is not.

Student 1: Thank you teacher and we love you too.

Student 2: And we are going to be like what you want us to be.

Teacher: Teddy! Why are sitting alone.

Teddy: *[silent]*

Teacher: Who wants to sit next to Teddy?

[The students laugh]

Student 1: No, he is dirty.

Teacher: No, don't say like that. Teddy... give me your copybook.

[Teddy brings his dirty copybook]

Teacher: What's this Teddy? You have to be neat. Tomorrow, I am going to see your homework.

[Teddy feels ashamed and nods his head. The bell rings. Students leave the class]

School principal: Miss Thompson! You need to have a look at the students' files to know more information about their progress.

Teacher: Yes, I have to.

School principal: So, here are the files.

She sits at her desk to read the students' files. She's shocked when she gets to Teddy's file.

Teacher: *[Reading..]* Teddy is a bright child with a ready laugh. He does his homework neatly and has good manners.....Teddy is excellent, well-liked by his classmates.....Teddy is getting confused because of the illness of his mother...... The death of Teddy's mother is affecting him badly.... Oh! Poor Teddy! *[in the classroom later]* Teddy! Show me your homework *[Teddy shows the teacher his book]* Wow! You're excellent Teddy. Your homework is neat. Thanks Teddy. *[She corrects his homework]* Ok students. Tomorrow is mother's day. I want you to prepare yourself to thank your mothers and I want you to consider me as your mother. Ok?

Students: Ok. *[The bell rings.]*

Teacher: Now you can go!

Narrator: The next day students bring presents for their teacher. All their presents are covered neatly except Teddy's present. The students give the teacher their presents. Teddy gives the teacher his present *[Students laugh]*

Teacher: *[opening the present]* Oh! It's so beautiful. Thank you, Teddy. *[The teacher puts on the necklace and the perfume that Teddy has given her]*

Teddy: Now I can see my mother and I can smell her too *[the teacher hugs Teddy and cries].*

Narrator: At the end of the year, Teddy passed his exams.

Teacher: Congratulations Teddy. *[Gives him his certificate]*

Teddy: I'll miss you Miss Thompson

Teacher: I'll miss you too Teddy. Take care of yourself.

Narrator: After 3 years Miss Thompson receives a letter

Teacher: *[reading]* I graduated from Prep school. *[she smiles]*

Narrator: After another 3 years.

Teacher: *[reading another letter]* I graduated from high school and now I am studying medicine at University *[to herself]* Wow! Bravo Teddy! *[reading again]* My wedding party is next week and I want you to come and sit at mother's place. *[smiling with tears]* *[at the party]* Teddy! Congratulations.

Teddy: Miss Thompson! You are the best teacher in my life. You are the reason for what I am now. Thank you Miss Thompson!

Teacher: *[with tears]* No Teddy. You are the one who has taught me how to be a teacher.

● ● ●

Saida says...

"It was a real pleasure for me and my students to participate in the playwriting competition. The students have gained lots of benefits through creating and performing the plays. They have become familiar with standing on the stage in front of others as they performed the plays in front of the school principal and some other teachers. This, of course, has increased their self- confidence. When I heard about the playmaking competition I decided to organise things in a way that could involve all the students in the school. So, I declared a competition for all students to write a short story in English with five characters or less. A lot of students participated and then I picked the best ones which I felt could be made into a play. I arranged a meeting with the students who wrote the best stories and discussed some ideas with them and with the school principal. As a result, we agreed to create and perform four plays including Teddy and Benjamin Carson as examples of famous people whose lives have changed because of good persons behind them. They started working in groups to turn the stories into plays. Most of this was done in the breaks between classes, using their own ideas, but they came to me to check things and sometimes I suggested modifications. It took about two weeks to agree on a final version of the scripts. Then we set up some after school sessions to rehearse the plays. The students who wrote the original four stories were given the chance to act in them more than others, and to choose who would play each part. Everyone was very enthusiastic during the whole process of making the play, I think because they had a specific goal that they were trying to achieve."

Us and Them

This play was created and performed by Reem Wadi,
Afnan Yehia, Deema Al-Mabhouh and Farah Al-Zain
from Beit Lahia Girls Prep School [A], Gaza with support
of their teacher, Mona Al Najar. A recording of the play
performed by the actors is available here....

https://youtu.be/X9mXSf1ef4Y

TV. Presenter: Hello and welcome to our Palestinian news channel. Today we are covering an event for a group of Palestinian girls talking to British people via Skype. Actually, it is about cultural differences. The British people as usual amazed us by their great civilization, hospitality and willingness to exchange knowledge with all people around the world. Now, our staff prepared this report 'Us and Them'. So, let's watch it!

Son: Hi, what are you doing ? Have you started without me? *[The son makes sure everything is ok and they're online via skype]* I think we are ready now.   Let's start!

Daughter: *[Talking to the British people via Skype]* Hello, dear! We are very proud of our heritage. As you can see we are putting on traditional dresses which are made of embroidery. This is a Kufia - a symbol of peace and Yasser Arafat. We are also famous for handcrafts like soap, pottery and ceramics.

Mother: Our food is very tasty like zaa'tar and olive oil which are very healthy. We have many traditional dishes like musakhan, maftool, hummus and olive oil. One of our famous Bedouin types of music is Dehiya.

Son: Let's dance some Dehiya! *[They all dance Dehiya together]*

Mother: What about sending our messages to them?

Son: Let's say our messages to them!

Son: I'm a Palestinian son. I study hard to be the first; to stand with my family and to serve my country.

Daughter: And I am a Palestinian daughter. All I need is a peaceful home, a toy and a flower. My dream is to grow up and gain some power, to free the people and Palestine together.

Mother: And I am the Palestinian mother. I feed, I clean, I sacrifice and I weep.

TV. Presenter: That was all for tonight. Thanks for watching!

●　　●　　●

Reem, Afnan, Deema and Farah say...

"The idea for our play, Us and Them, came from our need to share our cultural heritage with the world. But we believe that we need to be open-minded and look at differences too, so we decided to focus on talking to British people by Skype. We always love to do that. It gives us a chance to present a positive image of the Palestinians and send a positive message to the world. We like to communicate with people in other places and learn about their traditions and heritage. It's great to work together and practice English in a creative way."

Chapter 3

Freedom

More than 50 years of military occupation of the West Bank and more than 12 years of the blockade of Gaza have left a huge mark on Palestinian children, and understandably there were many plays submitted for the competition which had freedom for Palestinian people as a central theme. However there were also a large number of plays which looked at universal freedoms or the lack of freedom in other contexts. The first play here, **Rosa Parks drama,** looks at one landmark event in the ongoing battle against racism in the United States and **Left Behind** focuses on the lack of freedom to be a child experienced by so many children in poverty around the world. In **Break Free** and **When will the sun rise,** women's rights are explored; the context is Palestine but in fact these plays could be set in so many locations worldwide. **21 Hours** looks at what life is like for teenage boys in Gaza with only 3 hours of electricity a day, and **Beyond the Gate** and **Window onto the outside** show us some of the effects of being held in the huge open-air prison that is Gaza.

Rosa Parks Drama

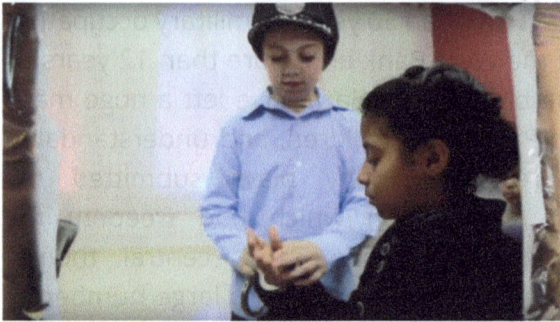

This play was created and performed by Nosiba Bilal Mohammed El-masri, Tasneem Abd el-salam Salem El-dabaji, Maria Ahmed Hamdi El. Masri, Farah Raed Mohammed Elsawarka, Nadeen Raed Salem El-hasanat from Beit Lahiya Elementary School with support from their teacher Miss Heba Hamouda. A recording of the actors performing the play is available here....

https://youtu.be/r2IqM-6iQLo

Scene one. A bus station. As was the norm in USA in 1955, black people sit at the back of the bus and white people sit at the front.

Bus driver: Ready? On your seats, please.

Scene two. A black girl sits opposite Rosa on a front seat. She is forced to move when a white girl, following her onto the bus, indicates that she must leave the seat. Another passenger gets onto the bus and stares at Rosa who is also sitting on a front seat.

White passenger: Hey negro lady! Go and sit at the back of the bus!

Rosa: No, I won't move.

The white man stares at her, astonished, and goes to tell the bus driver:

White passenger: There's a negro lady sitting on the front seat!

Bus driver: Where is she?!

White passenger: *[pointing at Rosa]* There!

Bus driver: *[shouting at Rosa]:* Hey negro lady! Go and sit at the back of the bus.

Rosa: No! I won't move. I won't leave my seat!

Another white passenger: Call the police! She's wasting our time.

Bus driver: *[looking threateningly at Rosa]* OK.....OK

A policeman comes to arrest Rosa. She drops her bag.

Scene three. While Rosa is in jail, demonstrations continue outside calling for her freedom.

Demonstrators: Free Rosa Parks! Free Rosa Parks!

At the same time, a boycott of public transportation has been announced. The bus driver looks sadly at his empty bus.

Scene four. The boycott leads to the end of racist division of seats. The passengers get onto the bus and sit wherever they like, regardless of their skin colour.

Bus driver: Ready? On your seats, please

● ● ●

Heba says...
"The members of our English club read the story of Rosa Parks and were inspired by her courage in seeking her rights. One of them suggested, performing the bus incident as our entry for the playwriting competition. The children were highly involved and interested in this unique experience. They became really enthusiastic about choosing the costumes and set, and commenting on each other's performances. And they got really excited when they heard that the judges enjoyed watching their play."

Left Behind

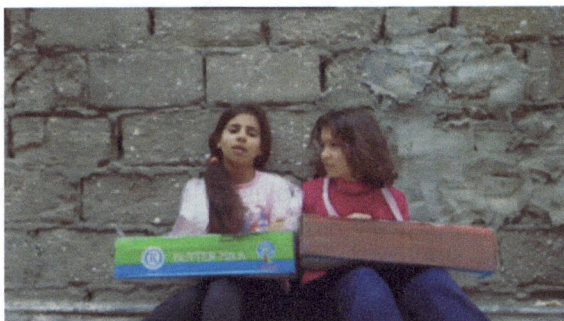

This play was created and performed by Deema Kahlout, Jana Herbawi and Tala abu Safi from Daraj [C] Elementary UNRWA School, Gaza with support from their teacher Samar Saleh. A recording of the play performed by the actors is available here...

https://youtu.be/X4eQF8oB_nQ

Two little girls are sitting beside each other on the roadway. They're cold and hungry and have boxes hanging around their necks.

Jana: It's cold. We've got to go home.

Dima : We can't go back! We didn't sell anything. How can mum cook for us if we don't bring money?! How can she get milk for our baby brother?!

Jana: *[sadly]* Oh! That's right. *[silence prevails the scene]* I wish I had a father who works and when he gets back from his work, brings delicious food with him. Don't other children live like that?

Dima: I wish I had the time for playing, watching TV, and going to school. And you know what? I want a coat coz I'm dying of cold.

Jana : I want to tell you something but promise me you won't laugh at me.

Dima: What?

Jana: I thought a lot! Till when shall we sell gum? Are we going to do this for the rest of our lives?

Dima: That's a tough question sister!

Jana: *[suddenly seeing somebody]* Look! Who's this?

Dima: Oh my God! Here comes our savior. Those rich men give a helping hand to poor people like us.

Jana: Then, he may help us.

Dima: Let's go and listen to what he's saying.

A man is standing in front of a podium, wearing a black suit, a hat and carrying a black bag in his hands. He's about to deliver a speech. He looks like a businessman or a politician. The two children are astonished.

The man: Hello everybody! It's my pleasure to be with you here today. I'd like to talk to you in the street in as much as I belong to you and you belong to me! I promise you to let the smile be drawn on your faces. No more tears ! No more coldness! There won't be working children. Children have to go to schools to learn and to be leaders of this nation.

The children are listening eagerly, imagining this to be true. He gives them both some gifts and pulls them towards him for a joint photo. Flashes of cameras are everywhere. The girls are happy.

The man: Say 'cheese'!

As soon as the cameras are gone everything changes.

The man: *[pushing the two girls brutally and taking back their gifts]* Go away!

The children are in a shock. They feel that they are left behind once again. They walk back to their place, carrying their boxes.

Dima: *[staring straight ahead]* The match seller died of cold then she became a legend. We're going to die of hunger and coldness. I bet no one will care.

Jana: Oh God! Give us patience, please. Give us strength to go on for our family.

Dima: *[to the audience]* Don't you dare say you can't do anything about it, because everything makes a difference. A word. A phrase. A thought. Just a sense of concern.

● ● ●

Samar says...
"In our school there are many children who work, and the girls who made the play often see their friends working after school. So they suggested the idea of making a play about this issue. The shocking thing is that even the 10 year old children who acted in this play, know that politicians are not always doing what they have to do. The children know that children having to work is a problem in many places and they felt immensely proud to know that their play has been seen by people all over the world."

Break Free

*This play was written and performed by Bissan Jamil,
Layan Said, Ro'a Zughayyer, Tina Toury and Yumna
Jabari from Muhammad Ali Al-Muhtasib High School,
Hebron with support from their teacher,
Maysa Qutteineh*

Scene 1. *At the meeting room. A self-confident lady in her early thirties, called Eve, is running a business meeting at the company she works for. She walks in to inform those working under her authority about the success that the company has been achieving recently. Employees are listening carefully to her remarks, nodding their heads and expressing astonishment.*

Narrator: Meet Eve, a successful young lady who managed to fulfil her dream of becoming the CEO of a major company in her country, Palestine. Her female colleagues consider her a role model to look up to. They always wonder about how she managed to be the person she is today. But the question is: Was it always the case for her? Let's see...

[As the NARRATOR stops talking, EVE ends the meeting]

Eve: Ok, that's it for today. We'll see you tomorrow to discuss other points.

[everyone leaves]

Scene 2. *In a kids' bedroom. Back in 1992, the five-year-old EVE was holding her Barbie doll and asking her eight-year-old brother, ADAM, to share some of his toys with her. ADAM enters the stage ahead of EVE and starts playing with his car.*

Eve: Adam! Come on! Let's share our toys.

Adam: *[shouting]* How many times do I have to tell you to go away? Can't this box process anything? *[pointing at her head]*

Eva: *[Speaking quietly with a sad tone]* I just want to play with your new car. It's so nice. You can play with my barbie too!

Adam: *[mocking]* Ha! Who wants to play with a stupid, pink dressed doll? *[stressing every adjective]* Plus, I want to know who are kitchen play-sets created for? Tell me! No, it's a rhetorical question!

Eve is sad and looks down on her way out of Adam's room. She drops her Barbie and Adam grabs it in anger.

Adam: Me, playing with this doll?? Hell no!

Adam exits the stage.

Scene 3. *In the living room. In 2002, EVE's mum is talking on the phone with her friend while ADAM, who is now a teenager, is leaving home and heading to the pitch for a football match.*

Mum: Really! ... Tell me more in details!

Adam: See you later Mum.

Mum: Bye honey. Take care! *[addressing her friend]* I was talking to Adam.

EVE is wearing sports clothes and is about to leave the house as well when she's stopped by her mother.

Eve: Bye Mum!

Mum: I'll call you back, OK? *[she hangs up the phone and approaches Eve]* I can see that you have been messing with your brother's clothes *[laughing]*

Eve: No Mum! *[enthusiastically]* School is running football trials today to choose new members for the women's football team and I am going for it!

Mum: What the hell are you saying? Are you out of your mind? You are not going anywhere sweetheart *[with a sense of contempt]* except for your bedroom. Go change your clothes because you look silly wearing them!

Eve: *[very disappointed]* I have been waiting for this chance for ages. You cannot simply make me miss the boat!

Mum: Well I guess I can and I will!

Eve: Mum, this is where I find myself and enjoy my time. This is...*[she sighs and thinks about what to say]* You know what? Why bother?

Eve goes back to her room, and Mum exits the stage complaining about her daughter's behaviour.

Scene 4. *In the living room. Three years later, Eve walks into the house holding an envelope and jumping out of happiness. Her Dad is reading a newspaper and is wondering why she looks so pleased.*

Eve: Dad, dad! I got the scholarship!

Dad: *[surprised]* What scholarship are you talking about?

Eve: *[very proud of herself]* I applied for a scholarship to study at Bethlehem University four months ago, and I have just been informed that I am accepted. Can you believe it?

Dad: Why study when you will end up in the kitchen, cooking dinner and washing dishes. That's what women do after all!

Eve: No, no. It's not what women do. Women have it all to become whatever they want to be. Women...

Dad: *[interrupting]* Don't argue!

Eve: Well, I am sorry. I have to argue this time because it's my future we are talking about right now. With all due respect Dad, I'm sick of you controlling my life. *[Decisively]* I'm not your puppet!

Dad: Your voice is getting too loud; behave yourself young lady *[goes back to reading]*

Eve: *[sarcastically]* Excuse me Dad, because for once I'm not going to remain silent while you think for me. I really apologize for misbehaving but enough is enough. I have zipped it up for so long. It is time for you to know that I am not less of a human being than you are. *[getting more emotional but less aggressive]* I want to fly Dad and you are weighing me down. All I'm asking for is an education, an opportunity to save myself. But, I guess I cannot do that without destroying the self you told me to be. I need your support Dad.

Dad thinks about what Eve has just said.

Dad: I have been mistaken all this time.

Eve and Dad hug.

Narrator: This is what Eve did. What about you girls? Speak out for yourselves because no one wins while standing still.

● ● ●

When Will the Sun Rise?

This play was created and performed by Reem Khalid Da'as, Manal Bassam Battah, Tuqa Ma'moun Khanem, Sarah Barakat Hamad, and Farah Isam Hamad from Hajjah Girls Secondary School, Qalqilia Palestine with the support of their teacher, Nasra Subhi Joma'h. A recording of the play performed by the actors is available here...

https://youtu.be/Qe0fDSB0qr4

[A mother and her two daughters in a living room].

Mother: My brother is arriving soon from Saudi Arabia.

Amal: He will be surprised that you can read and write. That you aren't illiterate any more.

[Shams, the other daughter, reads a headline from a newspaper]

Shams : A woman killed by her own brother. The cause of this crime is inheritance. Mum, why were you illiterate? And why did our dad leave us? And where did he go?

Mother: Sweetie, that was a terrible mistake done by my dad. He prevented me from going to school. Not only this, he also forced me to marry your dad when I was only fifteen.

[A young boy, the son called Ahmad, enters the room arrogantly and throws his school bag on the floor]

Mother: Why are you late?

Ahmad: Because the soldiers prevented me from reaching home.

Shams: Check points?

Ahmad: Yes, indeed!

Mother: Well, climb the wall as I did when I went to the literacy lessons.

[The mother used to climb the separation wall to go to her literacy lessons without her brother's knowledge]

Ahmad: Literacy lessons? Hahahahaha! ……. Amal , You… give me a cup of water!

Amal: But I am doing my homework now .

Shams: No, No, I will get you the water instead of her. Isn't it enough that you broke her hand?

Ahmad: No, I want her to get it for me. Shall I break yours too?

[He slaps Shams in the face]

Mother: Shams, he's your brother. Do what he asks you to do.

Shams : Mum....

Mother: Sweetie, this is what my grandmother, mum and I lived through. These are the customs and traditions. He's the man and we should carry out his orders. *[To Amal]* Do what he asks you to do!!! *[Amal, with a broken arm, gets Ahmad a cup of water but it slips from her hand and the water is spilled on him]*

Ahmad: Oh my God! What have you done?! *[Slaps her in the face]*

Amal: I'm sorry, I didn't mean it.

Mother: It's ok. It's ok. I will clean it. Don't worry. Don't worry.

Mother: *[There is a knock at the door]* It's your uncle. Look, don't tell him that I have learned to read and write. Ok?

Shams and Amal: Why?!

Mother: I will surprise him later. Ok?

Shams and Amal: Ok. *[Mother opens the door and welcomes her brother coming from Saudi Arabia].*

Mother: My brother! *[Takes his bag and kisses his hand]*

Uncle: My sister.

Mother: I missed you so much.

Uncle: Me too. Me too.

Mother : Why are you late ?

Uncle : The check points took a lot of my time.

Shams: Hello uncle.

Uncle: Hi.

Amal: Hello.

Uncle: Hi.

Uncle: Ahmad …. you're becoming a gentleman! How are you?

Ahmad: I'm fine uncle, fine.

Mother: How are you?

Uncle: I'm fine. And you?

Mother: I'm fine too. It's all right.

Uncle: Look my sister, I need your fingerprint on this paper.

Mother: Why?

Uncle: I want to take you to Saudi Arabia with me.

Mother: What!? It's ok. Why not?! I want to see the people and the places since I've never been abroad. It's my lucky day!

[He opens a paper and puts her thumb on an inkstand to put her fingerprint on the paper thinking that she is still illiterate.]

Uncle: Your finger…. *[Reading the paper, she finds out what the paper is really about. He wants her to give up her right to inheritance.]*

Mother: Oh my God!! You want me to give up my right to inheritance?

Uncle: How did you read it?!

Mother: It's my right. How could you?! How greedy and unjust you are!

Shams: What do you think of us? Do you think we are just goods for selling and buying? We're humans. We have rights exactly like you. No difference between a man and a woman.

Amal: Do what the Holy Quran and God ask you to do!

Uncle: Ahmad, teach your mother and sisters how to talk with men.

Ahmad: Nonsense!

Mother: My brother! Be fair! Be just!

The two daughters and their mother: We are victims of man's violence and brutality. Isn't it time to stop violence against women? When will the sun rise?

● ● ●

Nasra says...
"When will the sun rise" is a play written out of the suffering of Palestinian women. Women in Palestine are hard-working, devoted and peaceful but we face many obstacles in our lives; first and foremost the Israeli occupation and its injustice, and then our society itself. Writing this play benefitted my students so much, especially in their listening and speaking skills. Acting the play and rehearsing it many times enabled them to have the experience of being fluent and that gave them the confidence to act the play out in front of a huge audience. It was a great experience for me and also for my students."

21 Hours

21 Hours was written and performed by Osama Weshah, Ahmad el Lala, Ezz el Deen Bukheet, Adel Rajab and Yossif Kamel from Nusairat Prep [A] UNRWA School, Gaza.

Scene. The customers in the internet cafe are sitting waiting for the electricity to come back

Hammed is slowly combing his hair. Sameh is drawing a picture of David Beckham. Sari is holding his football and staring at it. Jasser is squeezing a nerve ball.

The waiter [Ramzi]: The location is an internet café in Gaza. The time is two thousand and seventeen. The electricity comes for 3 hours daily. From here begins the story. Bear with us...

Jasser: *[singing]* soon ... soon ... you'll taste my hell... soon ... soon ... you'll taste my hell... soon ... soon ... you'll taste my hell...

Hammed: Jasser! ...Enough .. You're getting on my nerves!

Jasser: Welcome to Gaza! Hahaha!

Sari: *[annoyed]*: You're such a boring person!

The waiter comes up to their table.

Ramzi: Hi guys ... What would you like to drink?

Hammed: Juice

Sameh: juice

Sari: juice

Jasser: Strong, thick, black coffee ...Haha!

Hammed: Seriously? ....Boring!!!

Everyone: Yes

Sameh: When will the electricity come back?

Ramzi: In about ... two hours..

Hammed: What are you saying? It's been off for 20 hours already!

Jasser: Welcome to Gaza ... Haha!

Everyone: Boring!!

Hammed: Do you want to do that puzzle game?

Sari: Of course not ..We're going to play Fifa 18 ... Have you forgotten?

Ramzi: Unfortunately, there are only two computers that can be used.

Hammed: Are you serious? How will we play?

Jasser: Why don't you play with me? [he mimes firing a gun and throwing a grenade]

Everyone: No, no ... That's sick... boring ....nasty!

Jasser: Cowards! ..Afraid of fighting!? .. Oh, how fun and amazing...

Everyone: It's boring ..sick.

Jasser: Then enjoy playing with your ball, my baby!

Sari: One day I'll be the number one footballer in the world.

Jasser: Haha! I'll cut my arm off if you become something ... You're just junk ...

Sari: You're just a piece of ...

Suddenly they are interrupted by the electricity coming back

Ramzi: *[shouting]* The electricity's back!

Everyone holds his joystick. Jasser plays a war game on one computer and the others play Fifa 18

Sari: Today..I am gonna score five goals

Hammed: We'll see..

Sameh: You'll see that I'm the best!

Sari: We've started!

Hammed: You won't do it!

Sameh: I'll do it .. Just watch.

Hammed: Pass to your friend ....come on .. Yeah, shoot! Come on! ... Goaaaal!.....Wow!...

Sameh: I did it .. I am the hero here!

The electricity keeps turning off and on irregularly.

Everyone: *[shouting]* No!!!! Oh my God....."

Sari: What happened?

Hammed: Is everything okay?

Sameh: Quick turn it on again!

Ramzi: *[stressed]* I'm trying ... I'm trying ...

Ramzi is trying desperately to fix their computer. Jasser's computer is the only that still works.

Ramzi: That's really bad! The power cuts have completely broken it.

Hammed: I hate Gaza!

Everyone: Calm down ..relax

Jasser: Come to me my darlings .. Here is the fun .. Here is the magnificence .. Kill him .... Taste my bombs ... it's wonderful...

Everyone is getting closer and closer to Jasser's computer one by one.

Sari: How do you throw a grenade?

Jasser: F5

Hammed: How does the knife movement work?

Jasser: F6 plus shift.....Game over!!! Who's the winner?

Ramzi: Wow! ... His blood has filled the whole screen.

Sameh: It's my turn

Hammed: No, It's mine.

Ramzi : Wait a minute ...it's still loading .. What would you like to drink?

Everyone: *[loudly]* Strong, thick, black coffee *[singing]* Soon ... soon ....you will taste my hell... Soon ... soon ....you will taste my hell...

Jasser moves towards the audience and slowly starts blowing up a ballon.

Everyone: *[loudly and pointing at Jasser]* Do you see ... if the darkness is our friend ... this is what will happen?

Jasser: *[singing alone and getting louder and louder]* Soon ... soon.....you will taste my hell.... Suddenly he stops singing and blows up the balloon until it bursts. Darkness.

● ● ●

Beyond the Gate

This play was created and performed by Raghad Abu-Shammala, Ghaida`a Abu-Dbaa, Fatima Shaat, Farah Almohtaseb, and Saja Al moghair, from Al-Madina Al-Munawarra UNRWA Prep Girls School, Gaza with support of their teacher, Hanan Hajaj.
A performance of the play by the actors
is available to view here..

https://youtu.be/WGdB-UyXSik

Scene. Ahmed rushes into the Palestinian waiting hall, speaking on his cell phone. His passport falls to the ground. He picks it up angrily, his eyes looking in every direction.

Sabra enters in her wheelchair, with a defiant face but tired body, carrying her medicine

Sabra: *[raising her hands]* Thank God! Finally in!

Leen: Oh God! I did it. *[She wipes the dust from her clothes and checks her papers]*

Wafaa: *[carrying her baby to her chest, with a cheerful face, speaking to her husband in Abu Dhabi on the phone].* We will gather soon.

Officer: Welcome! Please give me your passports.

Sabra: I am really exhausted and tired of taking medicine and waiting for chemical treatment abroad, but I still have hope to get it. We lack these things in the Gaza Strip, due to the siege, I hope this time I can travel. My life is in danger along with many other cases like me.

Leen: Oh! I hope my aunt you can travel and get your treatment. In fact, I got my scholarship abroad, one year ago, I did my best to convince my parents, to study abroad and I faced a lot of difficulties in getting this far. But as a girl I too have a right to choose what I want.

Sabra: Of course, you can do it. Have faith in yourself.

Leen: I will. I hope this time we can travel. Enough is enough.

Ahmed: Oh God! This is my last chance to resume my job, I am about to lose it as well as my residence in Abu-Dhabi. My boss sympathized with me, because of the siege, but I've been stuck here for over a year now. If I lose my job, I will lose everything. My mother is dreaming of doing a pilgrimage to Mecca. I'll lose my marriage and I won't be able to support my family. We have a very high unemployment rate in Gaza.

Wafaa: Oh dear! I too came from Abu-Dhabi, one year ago, to visit my sick mother. I gave birth to my baby here in Gaza. Even her father hasn't seen see her yet. I am desperate to see my son and my husband. I tried my best to travel but so far I couldn't. I hope this time I can.

Ahmed: You will. I will be by your side till you meet with your husband.

Wafaa: That's kind of you. I feel my case is like that of all Palestinians. Half of our people are refugees on the outside, and the rest are under the siege.

Ahmad: *[checking his phone]* Oh! Listen, listen! Breaking news, Rafah crossing point has just closed due to violence on the other side. What the hell!

Leen: I am about to catch my dream! This is so unfair.

Sabra: Oh God! I am going to die! Oh! I lost my last chance for treatment.

Wafaa: I cannot live without my family. It's a crime!

All together: We are the tale of the Gazan people who have suffered and are still suffering.

Officer: Cool down! What you did is in vain. You have to go back and register your names again. Take your passports.

All: It's our destiny as Gazan people to fall between violent actions on the other side and the siege. It's unfair practice not against Gazan people only, but against humanity.

● ● ●

Fatima's father, Marwan Shaat, who directed the play says..
"By doing the play, students gained the courage to stand on stage and to break the ice of hesitation, in delivering our message. 'Beyond the gate' was born from the suffering womb of the Gazan people. It was written to shed light on the hardships we face in all aspects of our lives caused by the ever-tightening siege. At the moment no one can leave, either through Rafah crossing or Erez. Many patients lost their lives. Many families are divided. Many employees lost their jobs. Many students lost their opportunities to study abroad and their visas. Many residents lost their citizenship. We want to tell the rest of the world what is going on in the Gaza Strip, to document the real history of Gazan people. We hope that people who call themselves supporters of human rights will stand beside us and really support us, saying loudly that enough is enough. We extend our hands to you in peace and harmony and we wish that one day peace will prevail in Palestine and the rest of the world."

Window onto the Outside

This play was created and performed by Diana Hadeehi, Monaliza Abo Seda, Tasneem Belbesie and Leena Zaqout from Mamounia prep UNRWA school, Gaza, with support from their teacher, Rana Musallam. A recording of the play being performed by the actors is available here..

https://youtu.be/byERDG9gntw

Narrator: Here we follow a story about two Gazan girls seeking their dreams, and the obstacles that hindered them from following them. These two girls had to travel to separate destinations to reach their dream but couldn't due to the blockade on Gaza. In an act of fate, the two girls met each other at the border and exchanged their hardships and stories.

Tasneem: *[singing]*

Liza: Wow! You've got an amazing voice. You should participate in a singing competition!

Tasneem: You've reminded me of my worries.

Liza: You look upset, what's wrong?

Tasneem: It's a long story.

Liza: No please, I would love to hear your story.

Tasneem: In the 2014 war on Gaza while I was at home a bomb struck and I was in a critical situation, and I lost my leg. Since then I've needed to go to Egypt to properly treat my wounds but I can't leave, and my condition is getting worse. My family and I tried with immense effort, but nothing worked to get me out of Gaza.

Liza: And why can't you get your treatment in Gaza?

Tasneem: Because I need an artificial leg, and that type of treatment simply isn't available in Gaza. I can see a lot of paintings with you. Are you an artist? Tell me your story.

Liza: Well, yes, I am an artist. I started painting when I was 13 years old, in the middle of the 2014 war on Gaza. I used painting as a way to vent out my sorrows. I drew the destruction of my town, and the painful state it left the people in. Through my paintings I showed the pain it is to live in Gaza, such as electricity shortages, lack of food and water. So, I started uploading my artwork on social media and soon enough I was getting attention from all over the world! I was lucky enough to be invited to travel to Britain for the opening of my exhibition, however I couldn't get out because of the siege on Gaza. People told me that my paintings were touching and inspiring. I wish one day I can stand with my paintings and meet my audience face to face and not only on social media.

Tasneem: Wow! That's an inspiring story!

Narrator: The two girls spoke about their life and dreams for hours when suddenly a TV reporter approached them after interviewing other people, and she came across Tasneem and Liza.

TV Reporter: We are now at the Rafah border where hundreds of people are waiting to depart Gaza for varying reasons such as medication, education, trade, and business. And we're here to interview these people. *[The reporter approaches Tasneem and Liza and starts interviewing them]*

Narrator: The two girls shared their stories and problems with the interviewer on television. The interviewer felt sorry for them and wanted to help the girls, so she promised to help them by starting an organization.

TV Reporter: After all these interviews with the Gazan people it is clear we all have dreams, even them. We need to send a message to the world to be merciful to the people of Gaza, as they are people too and require help. This is a call to everyone, please help the Gazan people. Open the borders and let them pursue their dreams! Leena Zaqoot, for Palestine news.

Narrator: The report went viral and the people empashised with the girls. People started reaching out and offering help. They set up an international organization and funds were set up to help the two girls and give them permission to leave Gaza safely. After some days, Tasneem was able to walk with an artificial leg and successfully participate in a singing competition. Liza was able to sell her paintings and become famous and both girls achieved their dreams.

All: *[chanting]*   Circle round for freedom

Circle round for peace

For all of us in prison

Circle for release

Circle for the planet

Circle for each soul

For all of our dear children

Keep the circle on

Keep the circle on

Keep the circle on

● ● ●

Rana says..

"We wanted to use our play to show the story of Gazan people wanting desperately to travel and not being able to make it because of the blockade. The play is based on a real story inspired by my 17 year old daughter, the artist Malak Mattar, who was invited to many exhibitions of her work overseas but, at the time we wrote the play, so far hadn't been able to travel. But the play represents the suffering of all Gazans who have their dreams and goals outside of Gaza, but whose dreams are never realised because of the blockade."

Chapter 4

Imagination

Despite the many hardships they face, Palestinian children continue to have hopes and dreams. In fact, many of the volunteers around the world who connect regularly to children in Palestine through the Hands Up Project are surprised by the enthusiasm and the willingness to connect that the children that they work with often have. Perhaps it is this ability to imagine a different reality that is the most powerful survival strategy that children in such a context can have. This idea is illustrated clearly in the first play in this section, **Hope**, the only play to reach the final stage of the competition that was acted entirely by boys. In **Sarah's Dream** and **I Have A Dream** we see some examples of this among children in very challenging circumstances; a child whose mother is dying, and children who live in an orphanage. **Hope**; **Tomorrow Is a Better Day** and **The Choice** emphasise the importance of positive thoughts as a way to bring about change, and in the last two plays, **Toothbrush** and **Inner Thoughts** we see how what is inside the mind of an individual isn't always what we might expect.

Hope

This play was created and performed by Ahmed Hatem Obaid, Mohammed Mohammed Shamieah, and Ahmed Ashraf Kuhail from Shohada'a El-Shikh Radwan Elementary School B, Gaza city with support from their teacher, Ashraf Ahmed Kuhail. A recording of the play performed by the actors is available here..

https://youtu.be/OZeEkdSbR_c

[Mohamad is building a model ship out of wood when Ahmed O and Ahmed K enter]

Ahmed O: Mohamed, what are you doing?

Mohamed: I am about to finish building my dreams ship.

Ahmed O: What?!!

Ahmed K: Are you serious?

Mohamed: Yes, I am. Does it sound strange?

Ahmed K: Of course it does.

Ahmed O: Palestinians don't dream my friend. Look around you, we live in dark. We can't travel.

Ahmed K: And we have lack in health care and education. We are under siege and know nothing about childhood

Ahmed O: We only know blood and wars. We are in Gaza. We are dead my dear.

[chanting]   Tears, blood, bombs and wars

                Pain and sadness inside doors

                Misery life and even more

                This is Gaza the land of sore

Mohamed: No my friends, No! Those who don't have hope will never make progress. We'll fight for our rights. And we must believe that one day our dreams will come true.

Ahmed O: Wow! That's inspiring..

Ahmed K: Thank you.

Mohamed: Let's dream together.

Ashraf says..

*"I had an amazing childhood in the land of dreams, Saudi Arabia.
My dad, may Allah bless his soul, used to ask me about my dreams
and wishes so he might help me to make them come true. He
taught me to be patient and fight to achieve what I want. Although
there were no barriers that may go against my dreams at that
time, he insisted that a person must try to achieve dreams himself
and never give up the struggles against the obstacles that may face
him. Nowadays, I'm a father of four children and I feel so sorry for
them since they live in one of the worst places all over the world to
have dreams in! Gaza has become a spot of frustration and
desperation for many reasons. However, I'm transferring what my
father taught me to my own kids, so that they may face the ugly
face of life in Gaza made by occupation. When I told Ahmed [my
elder son and one of the play actors] about the competition of the
hands up project, he insisted on doing something about his
dreams, so I encouraged him and we started writing the script
"hope" together. A final dream of mine is that my own children
can have a better life, and make all of their dreams come true."*

Sarah's Dream

This play was created and performed by Eman Hussam Musbah El-dadah, Deema Salah Musbah Mousa, Menna Mah, Jamal Arbid and Farah Salama Jamal Ajrami from Jabalia Elementary [A] UNRWA school with support from their teacher, Sarah Ismail. A recording of the play performed by the actors is available here..

https://youtu.be/NyBkHjBSo4s

A poor Gazan family with 3 daughters. The mum is sick, but can't travel to get the medicine she needs because the border is closed. Sarah and Deema are laughing, opening the pages of Sarah's drawing book. Her drawings are her dreams. The last page shows Sarah's biggest dream - the magic lantern. The poor girl realises that her dreams can't easily come true without a magic lantern. Deema is surprised by the magic lantern picture, and Sarah is embarrassed.

Mum: Children, children! Where are you children? Come and have your food..

[suddenly she collapses]

Deema: *[leaves her sister and rushes to her mum, lying on the floor]* : Mum...mum ....What happened mum...Wake up please....Are you kidding me ?? Mum....Mum.... I can't live without you ....*[Calling her sister]* ....Doa'a ...Where are you Doa'a.... Mum has fainted ....

Doa'a: Mum, Mum....Wake up Mum ...Mum....don't leave us.... don't leave me alone....Mum .. I need you ... I can't live without you .... I need a telephone .... Where is the telephone?? *[Telephone call with the ambulance]* Yes please .....my mum collapsed *[giving the address]* Jabalia 2nd Street. Come quickly please!

Sarah is standing, frozen, staring at them, frightened, desperate. She doesn't know what to do. She remembers the magic lantern in her picture. She runs to the kitchen and grabs the teapot. She calls the genie to come out.

Sarah: My mum needs to travel...she can't ...the border is closed....my dad can't find a good job ....He's out all day for just a few shekels....Come out!... Everything around me is disappearing....they even bombed the playground near our house..... I wish I could go with mum to a mall to buy toys, ice-cream, chocolate, biscuits....Is it such a big thing?!! Come out and tell me ....Come out and tell me... *[the electricity goes off]*

Electricity....I need electricity....I don't like candles.... I don't deserve it....I'm a good girl...I've heard of summer holidays, travelling from place to place .... from country to country....I want to visit Disney Land....I just want to play like any child in this world .....

I'm dreaming of a safe future , no wars , no bombs , no blood. *[there is the sound of an ambulance]* ....Mum ....Mum......I don't want anyone...I don't want anything .....I only want my mum.

●　　●　　●

I Have A Dream

This play was created and performed by Ahmed Al Jamal, Ahmed Hasanain, Ayl Abu Dobaa, Deema Muammar, and Nesma Al Haj Yousef from Rafah, Gaza with support of their teacher, Esraa El Shiqaqui. A performance of the play by the actors can be seen here..

https://youtu.be/3WnU4qgV6lM

Deema: *[reading a book and looking impressed]* When you want something, all the universe conspires in helping you to achieve it.

Nesma: That is true in case we are able to dream of something.

Ahmed J: And why don't we have the right to dream? We always have it.

Ahmed S: No one helps us in doing so. We are not able to dream because we don't have the most important thing in life - a family.

Ayl: Even if we don't have our own families, we should always dream. Losing our parents shouldn't deprive us from this simple right.

Ahmed J: I am sure every one of us has a dream hidden somewhere in his heart. And I have one too.

Nesma: Maybe yes we have. But we dare not let it out.

Ayl: At least, let's not be afraid and speak it out.

Deema: Can we pretend that airplanes in the night sky are like shooting stars? I could really use a wish right now. I've always dreamed of being a model.. lots of lights.. a massive number of people coming to watch me.. and many beautiful clothes that I can wear..

Ahmed J: I really wish to be a doctor. I'm dreaming of studying medicine from a high-ranked university. To be able to help people and heal them.

Ayl: I am always imagining myself as an astronaut. I wish to explore outer space.. to see the universe.. to look at earth from far away.. to see the stars..

Ahmed S *[looking with hope this time]*: I love music. I really wish to be a professional and famous musician. To let all my sorrows and pain out.. to turn my countries wounds into healing music.. to play music for the wounded and war dead.. to create beauty and to hear the applause that gives value to our work. And you Nesma.. won't you dream??

Nesma: I've always seen myself as a president. I wish to spread peace and end wars.. I want from all my heart to change my country to something better... to improve hospitals.. to make people work and earn money.. to make life worth living.

[All the children imagine themselves in these dreams. When they come back to reality, they see a real shooting star]

Nesma *[next to the window]*: come and have a look.

All the children go to see.. they smile with hope.

●　　●　　●

Nesma says..
"We were hoping that our greatest dream would be realized and that we would win the competition. I wanted to see what the outside world looked like and to see my brothers who are living abroad who I haven't seen for a very long time. Do you have freedom? Is it like our broken world? Every night I dreamed that I was sitting next to a window looking at the clouds and I wanted to touch them. But everything crashed when I knew we could not travel. My dreamy team was destroyed. We were always talking about our trip abroad. We were fighting about who would sit near the window of the plane and what we would bring to Nick as a gift from our land. All the team and I have a lot of dreams and put our great hope in the competition. We said that if we win it we will tell the world that despite the siege and despite the nightmares we are exposed to every night in the Gaza Strip, there are children here who have dreams of living freely and enjoying their rights. We in Gaza have the talent to write poetry and thoughts, but it's hard to find people who support us and stand for us. My greatest dream is to become the president of my country to spread peace and to help the children of my people realise their dreams."

The Choice

This play was created and performed by Razan Zomlot, Yousra, Mariam Masoud, Kefah Abu Aljedian and Marah Masaoud from Beit Lahiya Prep. Girls School [B], Gaza with support from their teacher Maisoon Shahada. A recording of the play performed by the actors is available here..

https://youtu.be/CJfwap-YvoE

Scene one. A husband and wife are in a living room. The husband is reading a book and the wife is sweeping the floor.

Husband: What will you cook today?

Wife: As always, nothing but cheese and bread.

Husband: Uffff! Ufff! What a life! No food, no food. Every day no food.

Wife: It's not my problem. You are lazy. Go out and find work.

Husband: You know there are no jobs.

Wife: A job is not a bird which will come and fly to you.

Husband: That's easy to say. Why don't you take my place and show me how you'll earn money.

Daughter: *[In her room, trying to study and talking to herself, sadly]* Every day the same; fighting, shouting, crashing! Nothing changes but the pain is getting worse. I can't bear it any more. I can't study. I can't sleep. I'm dying inside. I wish a miracle would happen and change my life.

There is a knock at the door is and the daughter goes to see who it is. She opens the door and two people are standing at the doorstep.

Richness: We are richness...

Love and peace: ...and love and peace.

Richness: We've chosen your house to make a change...

Love and peace: ..but you should choose one of us.

The parents hear this and rush towards the guests.

Husband: *[surprised]:* What are you saying? Are you serious? Is it true? Are you kidding?

The guests smile and nod their heads.

Wife: Thank God! Finally, money, food, clothes, everything we want. We'll be rich!

Parents: Of course, we'll choose richness.

Daughter: Stop. Stop! That's enough. I'm tired of you. You don't even notice me. You are selfish. You think of yourselves. I'm your daughter. Feel me. Love me. Take care of me.

Wife: Oh, my little daughter. The money is for you baby!

Daughter: I don't want money. I need your love. I need peace. I need to live happily with you. I hate fighting. I need peace dad! I need love mum!

Husband : But.........with money.. I can buy whatever you want.

There is the sound of bombing. The daughter hugs her dad.

Daughter: You can't buy me peace... I want to be safe... I want to be safe... I want to be safe..

Husband : OK... OK...calm down dear daughter.

Husband : *[to love and peace]:* We'll choose love for you my daughter. Come in Love and Peace. Welcome to our house. You are our guest. *[Love and Peace comes in and Richness comes too]*

Wife: *[to Richness]* And you?

Richness: Wherever Love and Peace go, I go too

Daughter: *[happily]* Trust me, Success will visit us too soon.

The mother wakes her daughter up. The daughter discovers that everything that has happened is a dream. Suddenly there is a knock at the door.

● ● ●

Hope: Tomorrow Is a Better Day

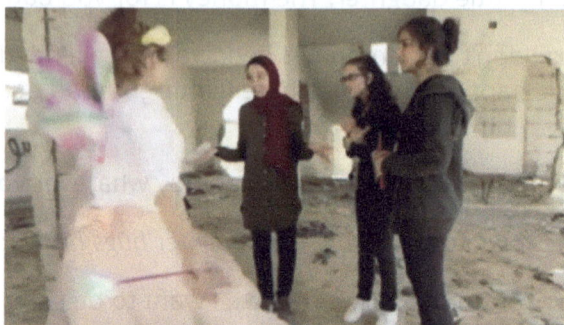

This play was created and performed by Mariam Al Shaer, Eva Safi, Lilya Mesleh, Marwa Shannan, Menna Al Batta from Al Rimal Prep [A] school, Gaza with support from their teacher, Fatma Al Jarrah. A recording of the play, performed by the actorsis available here..

https://youtu.be/ClHqVC-giaU

Scene 1. Four girls are standing motionless. They look so sad with pale faces. One girl is holding a candle [Eva] One girl is holding a broken toy [Menna] One girl is holding an empty bottle of water [Marwa] One girl is holding a picture of her dead father [Lilya]. The fairy appears, smiling and singing 'Tomorrow! The sun will come out tomorrow' [from the musical, Annie] She sprinkles fairy dust on the girls and at that moment, they come to life.

Scene 2. The four girls after coming to life are standing and wondering what happened to them. They are checking themselves, touching their faces and getting the dust off their clothes.

All girls: What's that? What's going on? Who is she? Is this a dream?

The Fairy: Pale faces, so sad but why?

Eva: Why? You think we chose this?

Menna: No... We were born like this!

Marwa: We've seen nothing but pain!

Lilya: What do you know about OUR life?

Eva: No light! no power.. Darkness became our only friend.. I don't like darkness.. I'm forced to live with it. I'm afraid of it.. I'm just scared!!!

Marwa: No power means no water!!! No water, no life. we struggle! We suffer! We are deprived from the life basics! And you're wondering why the sad faces? *[she sighs]*

Menna: All I want to do is to play in a safe place! A safe haven! No wars, no screaming or weeping over dead bodies.. No murdered childhood!!!

Fairy: *[shedding some tears]* And what about you girl? What do you have in your hands? You look the saddest among all?

Lilya: Me? What to say? What to tell? My life after I lost my father is like a hell!! Can you bring him back? No one will! His life was murdered! His smile was stolen.. I miss him! I wish I could have him back!

The 4 girls together: *[with some irony]* Did you get an answer for your WHY?!! This is our daily life.. We're like married to it! Why are we even talking to you!!

The Fairy: *[with a sad but firm tone of voice]* Losing a parent, a safe haven, and the life basics is something horrible. No one should go through it! But remember, life is all black and white.. If you let the black take over the white, agony and pain will be your friends forever.. So, get up, wipe away this sad look and try to create some hope.. Start from within.. Make the change you want to be.. seek the one person you wish to be.. Believe in tomorrow.. There will always be hope somewhere in this world!!! Just be that hope. Don't give up..

Come with me..

All girls together: But where?

Fairy: Just come!!

Scene 3. The fairy sprinkles some dust on them. The scene changes into a beautiful green land. The girls look so amazed with smiles on their faces. The fairy looks at them smiling as well.

Eva: Wow!

Menna: This is so beautiful!

Marwa: Amazing!

Lilya: This is life. This place is so colourful!

Fairy: Always be the change you want to be! Don't look back and let the past imprison your soul. You're young, you're strong and life is just ahead of you! This is just a test. Try to pass it!! And remember: tomorrow... *[she sings]* sing with me!!

The girls join the fairy in singing 'tomorrow, tomorrow, I love you tomorrow. You're always a day a way....'

•   •   •

Mariam, Eva, Lilya, Marwa and Menna say...

"To make this play we attended with Mr Nick a drama session. We loved it and we learnt many things about how drama could be done. Then after that we had a meeting and we agreed that the topic should be related to our life in Gaza or in Palestine in general. Then we started writing the script with help from our teacher. Then the final stage came and it's the most exciting one: the shooting. We're really proud of what we've achieved. Many people liked the play it and we loved doing it. This experience was one of the most inspiring and eye-opening we've had. We learnt how to write a script and we learnt that drama isn't only about reciting a script. It's also about applying our feelings and our senses. We learnt how collaboration and good team work can make everything go in a smooth and a perfect way. After we finished everything, and while training we became like a family and like sisters – especially with the big sister, our teacher, and I think that's the most important thing."

Toothbrush

This play was created and performed by Huda Abu Jarad, Marah al Tlouli, Areej Abu Jarad and Lama Ayoub from Khalil Oweida Prep. Girls School, Gaza with support from their teacher Hend Jawad Al Qattaa. A recording of the actors performing the play can be viewed here..

https://youtu.be/Zg51k7dGbl8

Scene one.
A mother and daughter are unpacking their bags.

The daughter: Mom...

The mother: Yes,....

The daughter: When's all this going to end? I'm tired of it!

The mother: Oh, baby! It will end soon. Don't worry! We're staying at your uncle's house. Maybe it's much safer here!

....

The daughter: Oh my God!

The mother: What?

The daughter: I forgot to bring my toothbrush!

The mother: So what?!

The daughter: Oh, mom! I can't sleep without brushing my teeth!

The mother: You must be kidding!

The daughter: I'll go to the shop nearby to get one! See you!

Scene two.
The daughter walks towards the shop. She freezes as she hears the sound of planes flying overhead. Areej comes and stands beside her. She walks around the frozen daughter as she narrates her thoughts.

Areej: And now, her life flashes before her eyes! All the sweet memories of her home! That place, near her home, where she was playing with her friends! Her bed and the photos she used to stick on it! The dining table that gathered the whole family and served their favourite food! Her teddy bear that she left on the bed! Her siblings who are living abroad and whom she can't see again! All the small things she left at home, here and there!

Scene three *[at the shop]*.

The daughter: Excuse me, sir! I need a toothbrush!

The shop keeper: What?!!

●　●　●

Hend says...
"We were talking about war in class one day and I asked the students about what they would miss if a war started again. All the things that Areej said were mentioned by the students and I told them about my own experiences during the 2014 bombing of Gaza. It happened that I actually lost my toothbrush during that war and I asked my father to bring me one if he could. I found nothing but the toothbrush to express the oppression that I felt at the time. So the play came out of this experience and the discussion I had with the students about it."

Inner Thoughts

This play was created and performed by Rawan
El Alawi, Dania Dahalan, Batool Sager, Salma
Shammout and Zaheya Arafa from New Khan Younis
Prep girls UNRWA school with support from their
teacher, Amal Mukhairez. A recording of the play
being performed by the actors is available here..

https://youtu.be/PypRVgj0S7E

The scene opens with a frozen image of three students. A girl enters talking to herself.

A: Wow! What a big house! What a beautiful garden! Why can't I have a big house like hers? Oh God! I love her large Barbie and her expensive phone. What if I were her....

[She freezes. The girl whom A was talking about comes to life.]

B: Yes! I have a big house with a beautiful garden... We spend our money on luxury cars, crazy parties and expensive vacations. But wait a minute! Can money buy health when it's lost? Our whole fortune couldn't help my mother when her body started to fail her. It couldn't ease any of her pains! I still remember her last minutes when she looked above her, then closed her eyes forever.

[B freezes. A comes to life.]

A: No, No, No! Thank God! I'm OK with my simple house. I have a beautiful caring mother! I'm so happy with what I have. *[A holds up a mirror and looks at herself]* Awfffff! I look terrible! I wish I was prettier! That girl I see every morning at the bus station. What if I had her eyes, her nose, her body. She's very beautiful!!

[A freezes. C comes to life. She says her lines using sign language.]

C: Don't judge a book by its cover. I am beautiful. That's true. I envy you though. You don't have to lip-read all the time. I can't laugh at jokes. I can't hear music. I only hear noise. Do you know how it feels to be deaf?

[C freezes. A comes to life again and rubs her ears.]

A: My ears! I have to be thankful! I am beautiful, aren't I?

[A pauses and thinks]

A: That new classmate! She's getting all the attention at school. Everyone is looking after her... teachers, students, even our school counsellor... but why? Why?.....

[A freezes again. D comes to life.]

D: Do you think I am happy with this? I lost my house, my school, my friends. Have you ever lived in a shelter? Do you have friends who lost their entire families in one airstrike? Have you ever thought that one of your friends might be buried somewhere under the ruins, waiting for help that may never come?! Have you ever closed your eyes, prayed and waited for death?

[D freezes. A shakes herself and sighs deeply.]

A: Oh! No! My! What's wrong with me? Why would I want to be like someone else? Why not accept who I am? God, you are so beautiful. You gave me so many beautiful things, so thank you.

[A looks at B, C and D]

A: My friends, in spite of everything, you are stronger than I thought! I've learned my lesson. Thank you. *[A looks at the audience]* And you! Your self-worth is determined by you! Love the person you are and make a difference!

●　　●　　●

Amal says...
"A good play tells people something about themselves. The more we can reflect on the human aspects in a play, the more we can produce a powerful, viable piece of work. That's exactly what we had in mind when we decided to participate in the Hands Up Project playwriting competition. We wanted our play to be about some basic things about humanity so that's where we started.

Students from different school clubs sat together to brainstorm what the play could be about before putting pen to paper. They gathered a list of beautiful stories, characters, problems, solutions, messages and settings. However, we only needed one good story, so the students decided that the play should highlight world issues, not only local ones, since it would be directed at a global audience, and it would be judged by judges from different parts of the globe with different cultural backgrounds. The students wanted their play to be globally understood so issues like refugees, wars, deafness, health, water and poverty were suggested as students believe that such issues matter to the whole world. Of course, in only five minutes we couldn't cover so many issues at once, so we limited ourselves to the ones which touched the students' everyday lives.

There was one main character and four secondary characters in the play. The main character of the play is not satisfied with the way she is, and envies others for what they apparently have. However, during the course of the play she realizes that each of them has their own problems, and that we shouldn't judge things simply by what we see on the outside. I think that the five characters produced a powerful performance, each one of them was a hero in her role. One of the elements which strengthens the play is the use of freeze frame and the moment when each character is brought to life is one of my favourite parts in the play. The idea of still images was suggested by Batool, one of the actors in the play, who was inspired by Nick Bilbrough's drama workshop in Rafah. Another innovative feature of the play was the use of sign language by Dania, who performed the role of the beautiful deaf girl. Using sign language seemed to be impossible at the beginning as no one at school knew this language but we visited a school for hearing and speech impaired people at the Palestine Red Crescent Society. There, Dania was trained in how to say her lines in sign language.

Playwriting is a great way to explore the inner thoughts and abilities that students may have. It's interesting to see how this experience has changed their attitudes towards each other and towards the world. I believe that they have learned how to express their local problems globally. They now understand that plays are created to be watched and heard, and the only way to make people hear you and watch you is to make yourself clear and understandable and relevant. "

From The Judges...

"I really enjoyed reading and watching these plays. It was wonderful to see such talent flourishing under such difficult circumstances."
Alexei Sayle, actor, comedian and writer

"A narrative of national struggle lasting 70 years presents both a challenge and an opportunity for storytellers. I was drawn to the plays that have given this ongoing story a new twist, and to those that identified other themes about choosing our own paths to happiness"
Andrew Foster, ex- English Projects Manager, British Council, Occupied Palestine

"It was incredibly hard to judge the entries for this competition as I was so impressed by many of the plays submitted. Watching the eventual winners perform their play 'Inner Thoughts' on stage at the Royal Theatre Stratford East alongside Mark Thomas - on only their second day outside of Gaza - was incredibly moving and deeply inspiring. The girls performed with grace, confidence and resilience - fully deserving the standing ovation they received at the end."
Colm Downes, English Project Manager, British Council, Occupied Palestine

"As a result of reading one of these plays, The adult English learners I teach from Japan and South Korea were inspired not only to perform their own version of one of them but also to create, perform and share their own short play. What could be better?"
David Heathfield, ELT author and storyteller, The University of Exeter

"A very impressive set of very different plays with some fabulous acting and some great scripts"
Fiona Copland, University of Stirling

"Judging the competition was for me both a moving and insightful experience. I am so glad to hear that thirty of the plays are going to be published. With good wishes and blessings to all of you who took part."
John Altman, actor, writer and singer.

"Being a judge for the play competition was an amazing experience. Huge congratulations to the Hands Up Project for getting so much involvement and enthusiasm for drama from so many different schools in Palestine."
Ken Wilson, ELT author and founding member of the English Teaching Theatre

'I watched the videos with my nine year old daughter. They spoke to both of us. We were moved, entertained, tickled and confused! Their humanity did this to us and there are many that will live long in the memory.'
Kevin Towl, ELT teacher, Santiago, Chile

"Taking part as a judge in this competition shed light on our pupils' amazing creativity and performance skills. The diversity of topics reflects the reality and our hope for a better future and it pushed them through this experience to confront and challenge themselves. Thanks very much for your efforts Nick Bilbrough in widening their scope and giving them this opportunity."
Kifah Sanori, English Education specialist, Palestininian MoE

"So many original, expressive, from-the-heart plays. Many examples of excellent team work, products of group creativity. Choosing the best ones was incredibly hard, they all deserve to be watched, listened to and appreciated."
Margit Szesztay, president IATEFL

"I was very touched by so many of the plays especially the ones coming from Gaza which talk about the dreams of girls and women"
Marina Barham, Director Al-Harah Theatre, Palestine

"It was such an honour to be able to watch these extraordinary plays and such a difficult task to pick a winner. They tell heart wrenching tales with profound messages full of hope, with impressive English language proficiency and creativity. They all deserve to win to be fair"
Nicky Francis, Women's centre manager, British Council, Saudi Arabia

"It was a real honour to be asked to be a judge. The experience was both heart-breaking and heart-warming. It was very upsetting to see how many children's stories were about the oppressive hardships no child should have to suffer. Nevertheless, there were moments that really made me smile, for example the young girl and her lost toothbrush. There was a clear feel from the plays that the indomitable spirit of the Palestinian people shines on."
Richard Chinn, Teacher Trainer, International House, London

"Attending many rehearsals for these plays, I saw the passion of the kids while working and how it was improving their language skills. This experience has empowered them with confidence and contributed hugely to their self-esteem."
Rida Thabet, Education specialist UNRWA Gaza and UNRWA TV

"Being Palestinian I assumed I could tell what the stories would be about. Having done it I realized I was wrong! Some of the topics as well as the views presented were unpredictable and in one or two cases controversial! This is the beauty I felt and I am grateful for what I learned!"
Salam Affouneh, Birzeit Univeristy, Palestine

"I would say judging kids' creativity was one of the hardest experiences I've had as many of the plays were worth watching and being the winners. However, it proved that Palestinian students and teachers are very innovative and deserve the world's attention and appreciation"
Shireen Irziqat, English Education Specialist, UNRWA Palestine

"Being a judge was a challenge and a memorable experience at the same time. A challenge because there were so many plays in the competition worthy of great praise. A memorable experience because I felt the depth and seriousness of the stories that were close to the authors' hearts and lives."
Stephan Breidbach, Humboldt University, Berlin

"The diversity in subject matter and the range of stylistic delivery exhibited by the young people in the play writing competition was quite astonishing. It was a privilege to be involved in this project. Witnessing this display of beautiful and inspiring creativity from a group of young people living with such adversity was truly humbling"
Tim Sayer, London School of Music

"A kaleidoscope of settings: living room, schoolroom, woodwork room, street, olive grove, border crossing; of emotions: friendship, love, hate, loyalty, jealousy, empathy, fear, terror, resignation, but above all, hope. Each play an insight into young people's lives in Palestine"
Jane Willis, ELT author

"Writing a play and putting yourself in the place of other people is probably one of the hardest forms of art there is as you need to show empathy to different situations. I hope that some of the work the students did in the course book helped to get them to be able to get their ideas onto paper. Mabrouk!"
Wendy Arnold, author of English for Palestine [Grades 1 to 6]